Asher Reich

This book was made possible through cooperation
between the University of Wisconsin Press and
the University of Wisconsin–Milwaukee
Center for Jewish Studies.

Asher Reich

Portrait of a Hebrew Poet

Yair Mazor

Illustrations by

Michael Kovner

THE UNIVERSITY OF WISCONSIN PRESS

The University of Wisconsin Press
1930 Monroe Street
Madison, Wisconsin 53711

www.wisc.edu/wisconsinpress/

3 Henrietta Street
London WC2E 8LU, England

1   3   5   4   2

Printed in the United States of America

Library of Congress Cataloging-in-Publication Data
Mazor, Yair, 1950–. The poetry of Asher Reich: portrait of a Hebrew poet /
Yair Mazor; illustrations by Michael Kovner.
       p.   cm.
Includes index.
ISBN 0-299-18150-2 (cloth: alk. paper)
ISBN 0-299-18154-5 (pbk.: alk. paper)
1. Reich, Asher, 1937– —Criticism and interpretation.
I. Kovner, Michael, 1948–   II. Title.
       PJ5054.R389 Z63   2003
   892.4′16—dc21   2003005679

For YAEL, my daughter,
for BILHA, my wife,
and for RACHEL and ITZHAK,
my late, eternally remembered parents.

Tender is your love.

and for
SARAH ROSENTZWEIG
whose love and devotion, support and affection
everlastingly rest, nest, in my heart.

What are we without our
Loved ones
Without our love
Without our memories
Good and bad
Without our yearnings
Missed and met.

Y. M.

Contents

Illustrations

Asher Reich

Asher Reich

No Fear of Flame

Asher Reich is a prominent and fascinating voice in the intricate choir of contemporary Hebrew/Israeli poetry. Born in Jerusalem in 1937, he is firmly rooted in the cultural landscape of Israel's secular society—which has enthusiastically absorbed the artistic values of America and Europe—although he was educated in a religious, orthodox Jewish school and yeshiva until the age of eighteen. Reich's colorful and expressionistic poetry faithfully reflects the dual strands of his biography. Conservative past meets the defiant, liberal secular present, and layers of Jewish sources—the Bible, the Talmud, the Torah, pious prayers, folk tales, and aphorisms—interlace with modern Western values in art, culture, and philosophy. In Reich's poetry, polar opposites meet and yield a uniquely colorful and rich texture. If a flame is a metaphor for fervent passion, vitality, and sensuality, then Asher Reich's poetry can be described as one that plausibly displays fervent love forever and never fears flame.

Recognition came early, in 1961, when he won the Anne Frank Award from the America-Israel Cultural Foundation. His first published volume of poetry, *On the Seventh Year of My Wanderings* (1962), marked his arrival as a contemporary Hebrew/Israeli poet. His second volume, *A Nocturnal Sunrise* (1969), won a distinguished prize from the Israeli Association of Artists, Composers, and Writers. More volumes of poetry followed: *The State of Affairs* (1975), *A Reference* (1978), *Women's Tractate* (1980), *A New Packet* (1983), *Table of Contents* (1983; awarded the Bernstein Prize of the Federation of Israeli Publishers), *Works on Paper* (1988), *Fictional Facts* (1993), *Winter Music* (1996), *The Face of Earth* (1999), and *Lifeless Future* (2003). Other awards include the Israeli Prime Minister Prize for Poetry (1989), a DAAD (German Academic Exchange Service) scholarship in Berlin (1990), Tel Aviv Award for poetry (1992), and Israel's President Prize (2000). In 1999, Reich was elected to the German Academy of Poetry and Languages. And in 2000 he was given the Poetry Prize by the city of Basel, Switzerland.

Reich's poetry has been translated into twenty languages. Toulouse Press published a volume of his poetry in French in 1980. *Works on Paper* was published in German *(Arbeit auf Papier)* in 1992, and *Winter Music* is forthcoming in German, both by Rowhot Press. Reich's novel, *Memoirs of an Amnesiac,* is currently in press in German translation by Bleicher Publishing House.

Reich also writes prose fiction. His novel, *Memoirs of an Amnesiac,* was published in 1997, and his volume of short stories, *A Man with a Door,* is currently in press. He was editor-in-chief of *Moznayim,* a monthly literary periodical of the Israeli Association of Writers. He has taught creative writing in various academic institutions, including Ben Gurion University in Beer Sheva. He lives in Israel.

Michael Kovner

A Painter of Many Colors; or, Abstract Does Not Live Here Anymore

Michael Kovner was born in 1948 on Kibbutz Ein-Hachoresh ("Spring of the plower") in the sylvan part of the Galilee.[1] After completing his military service in the paratroopers' elite commando squad (under Ehud Barak, who became chief of staff of the Israeli army and later prime minister of Israel), Kovner studied art, painting, and drawing at the New York Studio School under Philip Guston, Mercedes Matter, and Steven Sloman. He is one of Israel's most gifted artists.

Kovner did not surrender to the sweeping postmodernist spirit of perplexing abstract and nonfigurative painting associated with such styles as minimalist art, *Arte Povera* (poor art), and conceptual art. Rather, his work has a figurative, lyrical touch that corresponds to

French fauvism (a branch of French impressionism), to postimpressionism, and to some extent to cubism. His works cover such wide-ranging themes and subjects as Israeli landscapes, evincing some influence of cubism; tenderly erotic female figures, often reminiscent of Edvard Munch's dusky, murky expressionistic paintings; urban sites and still life, which seem to marry a fauvist touch with urban futurism and Paul Cezanne's commencing cubist inclinations; and "untamed" nature, which reveals a singularly personal and intimate style of postimpressionism. In no way diminishing Kovner's originality, the artistic influences that his art has enlisted, absorbed, and internalized have acted as an Archimedan point, a "goading trigger," a springboard from which his art tracks, invents, cultivates, and fashions its unique artistic handwriting.

Kovner's work has been shown in museums and galleries in Israel and abroad. His one-person exhibitions have included "Paintings from New York" (Artists House, Jerusalem, 1978), "Landscape Drawings: From Flying Bird's Perspective" (Binet Gallery, Tel Aviv, 1979), "Old Desert Paintings" (Binet Gallery, 1981), "Houses in Gaza" (Binet, 1983), "Images: Painting Inspired by Lego" (Gordon Gallery, Tel Aviv, 1985), "Meet an Israeli Artist" (Israel Museum, Jerusalem, 1988), "Portraits" (Binet, 1988), "Landscapes" (Binet, 1990), "Jerusalem Scenes" (Binet, 1992), "A Girl in a Room" (Binet, 1995), and "End of the Year 1995" (Binet, 1996; NAFI Gallery, New York, 1997; and Yale University, 1997). His works have appeared in such group exhibitions as "A Turning Point: Twelve Israeli Artists" (Israel Museum, Jerusalem, 1987), "Towards a New Realism" (Ashdot-Ya'akov museum, near the Sea of Galilee, 1988), "Fresh Paint: The Younger Generation of Painters in Israel" (Tel Aviv Museum of Art, 1992), "A Tribute to Ayala" (Israel Museum, Jerusalem, 1995; Ramat Gan Museum of Israeli Art, 1997), "Landscapes" (Ramat Gan Museum of Israeli Art, 1997), and "Port" (Haifa Art Museum, 1998).

The artistic evolution of Kovner's paintings and drawings was motivated by ideology. It seems to have begun during the mid-1970s, after a long stay in southern France and Italy amid traditional art and painting, when Kovner concluded that the fashion of abstract painting had come to a dead end.[2] His conclusion proved beneficial, for it enabled him to develop to the fullest his personal artistic potential and to mark his own unique territory in the artistic landscape of contemporary Israeli painting, which tends toward abstract and deliberately obscure "conceptual art" and "minimalist art."

Many of Kovner's early paintings (from the mid-1970s through the eighties) portray stark landscapes of the Israeli desert, the mountains surrounding Jerusalem, or wooded sites in Jerusalem. They use striking colors, which seem to enhance the landscape's tempestuous, even turbulent quality, its restless, relentless movements. These landscapes strongly emphasize the outlines of steep slopes, stones, rocks, and trees, echoing Vincent Van Gogh's piercing forcefulness, yet bestowing a touch of assertive expressionism as well as bold, vibrant impressionism and postimpressionism. Other paintings portray buildings in semirural landscapes, which seem to reflect several influences. While the bold colors bring to mind French fauvism (for instance, Henri Matisse, Raoul Dufy's beaming color spectrum, or Robert Delaunay), the objects (mostly houses) tend to echo the cubist, plain architecture of the German Bauhaus style, tinted by a Middle Eastern atmosphere that corresponds to Giorgio de Chirico's and Edward Hopper's cold surrealism. The fingerprints of de Chirico and Hopper are particularly visible in Kovner's paintings of the eighties, which present toys, shop windows, and other objects in a surrealistic atmosphere of cold, dreamlike alienation and a scary, even nightmarish ambience. In his series of portraits (1985), Kovner displays a skillful and delightful ability to incorporate various artistic sources in his own innovative work. Thus, the colorful portraits

Morose Realism

combine salient fauvist elements (cheerful and welcoming in their radiant, glowing colors and flowery backgrounds) with earnest-looking expressionism that focuses on the inner message as forcefully conveyed by the person's (usually female) stern personality.

Kovner's paintings of the nineties range from landscapes to cityscapes. Some document industrial urban sites, mixing "round cubism" (such as Fernand Léger's) with a strong visual technological message that brings to mind Italian futurism. Many of them capture both a single passing moment and an ongoing mood; they bear the colorful footprints of Raoul Dufy, Paul Gauguin, Amedeo Modigliani, and Henri Matisse, while suggesting at least a hint of the somber loneliness and alienated gloom and doom of Edvard Munch. Other landscapes—many of them portraying semirustic, semiurban land-scapes of small towns with small houses and slanted roofs—pay homage to Cezanne's first hesitant, "groping," "fumbling" steps to-ward cubism. Yet their colors seem to deviate deliberately from real-ism (at least realism that is typical of Israeli scenery), using vivid, re-vealing, vivacious, bold brightness. Kovner's other paintings of the mid-1990s tend to return to "netted nature," focusing closely on mountainous landscapes, cows in the meadows, and herons in pas-tures. These somewhat robust, earnest-looking paintings skillfully convey a sense of profound rootedness and vivid vitality.

Etchings and charcoal works by Kovner from the nineties also tend toward the earnest, documenting the internal, dramatic mo-tion of nature in its everlasting movement and vital struggle. Main-taining the figurative element as the cornerstone of his artistic evolu-tion (in which landscapes and women play prominent roles), he moves to and from a variety of artistic schools, absorbing from each the qualities that are in aesthetic congruence with his own unique, artistic inclinations. Combining characteristics of different schools of art, he produces a striking mixture that feeds and fortifies his own artistic goals. He skillfully enlists all those influences as inspiration, though they never eclipse or cloud his own originality but rather re-lease and enhance it, channeling it through his unique route of ex-pression. While Kovner's art faithfully adheres to reality, he often goes beyond the depicted reality, using it as a prism or a medium through which to convey his own message. That message succeeds in expressing both a personal, intimate interpretation of the depicted reality and its universal, humanistic values. Thus, Michael Kovner's "refusal" to surrender to the sweeping fashion of artistic abstract and postmodernist trends has done excellent service to his own, private artistic genius as well as making a great contribution to contempo-rary Israeli art.

To Be or Not to Be Is Not the Question

How to Be and How Not to Be Is Both the Question and the Answer

> Sherlock Holmes weighed every particle of evidence, constructed
> alternative theories, balanced one against the other, and made up
> his mind as to which points were essential and which immaterial.
>
> *Arthur Conan Doyle,* The Hound of the Baskervilles

This passage from *The Hound of the Baskervilles* serves as a metaphor
for my intellectual and scholarly credo. The way in which Sherlock
Holmes operates rationally when attempting to decipher a mystery
and decode and crack a challenging case is a process upon which
comprehensive scientific analysis must be founded.

Regretably, too many people fail to comprehend the correct concept of science and its very essence. They operate on the false assumption that "science" is associated with fields of study such as chemistry, physics, biology, zoology, and mathematics, to the exclusion of the humanities. This is wrong. Science is not a specific field of study but rather a specific mode of investigative procedure. Physics is not science. Chemistry is not science. And biology is not science. Likewise, history, literature, and sociology are not sciences, nor is any other field of human knowledge. However, they all turn into science when they are investigated by a scientific method.

What is a scientific method? A scientific method attempts to portray and map a certain "slice" of reality (history, biology, philosophy, chemistry, physics, literature, et cetera) while developing and cultivating a theory regarding the corpus in focus. It considers not only the subject's external stratum but also its internal, hidden stratum and the ways components of the comprehensive, bi-level structure interact. Hence, the theory may be compared to an x-ray that aims to reveal the internal "cryptic" parts deeply embedded in the whole, while examining and understanding how they coexist, interact, and form the "whole." The theory can be either verified or proven wrong.

Thus, in order to test the theory, the scientific method develops a methodology consisting of a cluster of inspecting devices. A precise and careful use of the methodology, while applied to the corpus in focus, should yield the desired results: the theory will be proven valid or erroneous. If the theory proves cogent, it can be further developed with new and innovative hypotheses regarding the corpus's characteristics and avenues of operation. If the theory fails, however, the researcher is compelled to return to square one. The researcher must dismiss the false theory and develop and test a new one. Only the scientific method can turn any field of knowledge and intellectual curiosity into science. Only this process turns physics into science or literature into science. Once physics and literature are subjected to the scientific method, they are translated into the science of physics and the science of literature. Thus, the question is not "to be or not to be." "How to be and how not to be" is both the question and the answer: how to be a scientist and how not to be a scientist.

Indeed, the theories and methodologies of the science of physics are dramatically more complex and precise than those of the science of literature. But that is a normative, judgmental matter that does not deny the essence of the science of literature, one that is an objective and descriptive matter (although its corpus consists of subjective raw materials). A judgmental observation and an objective matter are entirely different from each other, like two parallel lines that never meet. The quality of an object neither affects nor converts the objective and descriptive nature of that object. For instance, a chair does not stop being a chair if it is rickety and causes an aggravating lower back pain. A work of art does not stop being a work of art if it fails to meet the aesthetic standards of the *Mona Lisa*. Aristotle is dear to me. So is Plato. But the truth is even dearer to me. The fact that I am not the first who formulates the truth does not detract from truthfulness. I am the first to confess that although the theories and methodologies of the science of physics are significantly more complex than the theories of the science of literature, I still take pride in being a literary scientist.

Fervent Love Forever

Asher Reich's Poetic Portrait
and Its Prominent Role
in Contemporary Hebrew Poetry

Asher Reich's poetry, with its unique aesthetic characteristics, plays a central role in contemporary Hebrew poetry. To appreciate that role, it is first necessary to discuss some of the most conspicuous aesthetic characteristics of contemporary Hebrew/Israeli poetry. Approaching Reich's poetry in that context will shed more light upon his aesthetic genius.

The aesthetic credo of contemporary Hebrew/Israeli poetry was crystallized in the 1960s—the decade in which Reich's poetry budded, blossomed, and began gathering literary momentum—after its incubation period in the early fifties. During the fifties, such poets as Nathan Zach, Yehuda Amichai, and others who formed the literary group and wrote for the literary journal *Likrat,* along with poets

Moshe Ben-Shaul, Avner Treinin, Moshe Dor, and others, began fashioning a new aesthetic agenda for modern Hebrew poetry. These young poets were profoundly influenced by Anglo-American imagists (early Ezra Pound, Amy Lowell, Hilda Doolittle [H.D.], T. E. Hulme, Richard Aldington, and others), by their American successors (Wallace Stevens, William Carlos Williams, e. e. cummings), by Russian acmeism (Nikolai Gumilev, Osip Mandelstam, Anna Akhmatova), and by the Hebrew poets David Fogel and David Avidan (the aesthetic anarchist who conducted a poetic interaction with *Likrat*).

Despite aesthetic differences among those influences, these poets shared some common denominators, which fed and inspired the new poetic agenda and the aesthetic manifesto created by Zach, Amichai, Avidan, and other *Likrat* poets. Among those common denominators were a modest choice of themes, which focused on mundane, everyday, common topics; subdued, understated rhetoric; simplicity of style and syntactical patterns; a humble point of view by the poem's narrator; avoidance of complex, intricate patterns of rhyme and meter; and a general tone of meekness. All those qualities were cultivated as rejection of and protest against flowery, "tempestuous," and complex symbolism—poetry that sacrificed the individual voice on the altar of celebrated, symbolistic ideas and manifested itself by "thundering loudspeakers," dramatic gestures, sweeping rhetoric, ramiform metaphorical complexity, and themes and ideology bigger than life that flaunted grandeur and glory, intense flames and dazzling fireworks.

Thus, an aesthetic agenda was created, cultivated, and practiced by Anglo-American imagism and its American followers, by Russian acmeism, and by David Fogel, in the second and third decades of the twentieth century. Fogel's mentor was the Hebrew poet Abraham Ben-Itzhak (Sonah). They both presented an alternative poetic credo, one that preferred meekness and whispers to overwhelming

All Drums Had Died

echoes of roaring drums, modest simplicity to sweeping complexity; it cherished the lost, confused, and perplexed individual and abandoned "the sound and the fury" of ideological certainty. The imagists, the acmeists, and Fogel all fostered humanism and centered on the well-being of the individual.

Two leading poets, Abraham Shlonsky (1900–1973) and Nathan Alterman (1910–1970), dramatically dominated modern Hebrew poetry like unchallenged tyrants from the early thirties through the early fifties. Both were ardent and enthusiastic disciples of Russian and French symbolism (Shlonsky, to some extent, was also a pious adherent of Russian futurism). Both produced symbolist poetry saturated with clusters of convoluted flowery, metaphorical paradigms, with intricate and cryptic networks of themes and ideas, wrapped up in pedantic structured patterns of rhyme, meter, and rhythm. During Shlonsky's and Alterman's reign over modern Hebrew poetry, Israel was struggling for national independence and fighting for its very physical existence. The national struggle naturally put the collective interest in the forefront and relegated the individual to the rear. Also, in symbolist poetry, themes, ideas, and ideology (while being covered under vibrant metaphors, both colorful and opaque) always eclipse the marginal individual. In this respect, Shlonsky and Alterman's symbolist credo, one that clouded the individual in the name of the idea, was in congruence with the Israeli national reality, which preferred collectivity over individualism.

The revolt of Zach, Amichai, Avidan, and the *Likrat* literary group against Shlonsky and Alterman's school of symbolism was reinforced by their strong rejection of the emphasis on national collectivity and ideological proclivities at the expense of individualism. In the mid-1950s, when the struggle for independence was over, Israeli society turned from aspiration, hope, and dream to an everyday, mundane practical reality. Thus, although the state was in no way free of challenges and difficulties, the collective national goal of statehood and independence had been achieved.

Since art and literature tend to respond aesthetically to reality—mirroring it, interpreting it, challenging it—the early fifties marked a temporal turning point. The time was ripe to abandon the literary and poetic dedication to national issues and to start focusing on the individual: the outsider, the lost one, the complex one, the perplexed one, the disoriented one (to a great extent inspired by the literary works of Franz Kafka, Albert Camus, and the existentialist and absurdist trends in belles lettres philosophy). Zach, Amichai, Avidan, and other *Likrat* poets were young, hungry, energetic, and ambitious, filled with a fervent desire to blaze their own path in the "republic" of modern Hebrew poetry. They armed themselves with the teachings of those who preached the "aesthetics of austerity," and they were ready to divorce themselves from collective national themes. Thus, they launched their revolt against the tyranny of Shlonsky's and Alterman's symbolism. The aesthetic revolt that started in the fifties came to full fruition during the sixties. No wonder, as those were years of political, cultural, and emotional turmoil in the United States (the Vietnam War and the "flower children's" rebellion) and Western Europe that soon reached Israel (although differently).

That aesthetic revolt may be considered the dividing line between modern Hebrew literature and contemporary Israeli literature. A similar revolt occurred in the realm of prose, when Amos Oz, A. B. Yehoshua, Aharon Appelfeld, and Amalia Cahana-Carmon emerged on the scene in the early sixties and rebelled against their predecessors' preoccupation with national collective aesthetics (which stemmed from the national reality of the war for independence, one that demanded "fortified" collectivity), focusing instead on the perplexed, lost individual who roams a world bedeviled by chaos and absurdity. Similarly, contemporary Hebrew/Israeli poetry left the cradle in the early fifties, defined its boundaries from the mid-1950s through the early sixties, and reached full artistic maturity during the late sixties. Among the many poets who participated in that aesthetic process of incubation and creation, Nathan Zach was the leading figure. In both his poetry and his essays he formulated and designed the aesthetic manifesto of contemporary Hebrew/Israeli poetry.[1]

Nathan Zach (1930–) conceived and shaped his poetic credo while leading the passionate mutiny against the symbolist poetry of Shlonsky and Alterman. He was inspired by David Fogel (1891–1944), whose "aesthetics of austerity" and undertone were blatantly repudiated by Shlonsky and Alterman. Poetry was experiencing a domino effect. In order to fully appreciate the aesthetic spectrum of Hebrew/Israeli poetry in the sixties, one must know about Nathan Zach's aesthetic manifesto and practice. And, in order to relate accurately to Nathan Zach's poetic credo, one must know about the poetic credo of David Fogel, the one on which Zach founded his own. Zach was the herald who delivered the "aesthetics of austerity" to modern Hebrew poetry and its master, but Fogel was not only its harbinger, he also provided its quarry and raw materials.

Indeed, Fogel was not acquainted with the term "aesthetics of austerity."[2] It is a term I coined to describe poetry that adopts simplicity of structures, a modicum of symbolism, humble language patterns, and subdued rhetoric. However, the term itself is marginal in comparison with the content, the semantically signified entity that it denotes and marks. Hence, terminology is nothing but a means of effectively practiced communication that relates to paramount and significant issues under discussion.

The term "aesthetics of austerity," or, perhaps the "poetics of poverty," at least as verbal combinations, seem to be an oxymoron: a self-contradictory expression. Poetry, literature, belles lettres are expected to reflect literary plenty, aesthetic complexity, bountiful poetic richness. Yet, the aesthetics of austerity is not at odds with aesthetic complexity, nor does it negate worthy literary qualities. Lofty metaphors, elevated rhetoric, ramiform symbolism, and intricate patterns of structure are not the only ways to achieve laudable literary values. Some of Ezra Pound's works, those of William Carlos Williams, or Japanese *haiku* poetry illustrate this, amply. When skillfully executed, poetic restraint can produce works of praiseworthy value.

Three Millennia of Hebrew Poetry

The aesthetics of austerity is a recent development in Hebrew poetry, which is three thousand years old. Hebrew poetry began in the Bible and led to secular and liturgical poetry in the times of the Mishnah and Talmud (commentaries on Jewish Law, as introduced in the Torah/Pentateuch, the five books of Moses); medieval poetry in Spain (both secular and liturgical); poetry of the Enlightenment *(Haskalah)* in Italy, Austria, Poland, and Russia, in the eighteenth and nineteenth centuries; the Revival *(Hatechiya)* poetry in Eastern Europe at the dawn of the twentieth century; and modern poetry in the land of Israel since the early 1920s with the works of Hayyim (Chaim) Bialik, Sha'ul Tchernichovsky, Abraham Shlonsky, Nathan Alterman, and others. Despite conspicuous differences among these types and periods of poetry and aesthetic schools spanning hundreds of generations, they share one common denominator: aesthetic richness. None of them is marked by the aesthetics of austerity. Indeed, each of those literary periods exhibits its unique version of structural complexity, lofty metaphorical patterns, abundant and varied diction, and elevated rhetoric; in each, the poetic richness and variety evolved from differences in cultural circumstances.

In each of those literary periods, the lack of aesthetics of austerity is evident and obvious. Every literary creation may be metaphorically described in chemical terms as a molecule, which is founded on the following two interacting atoms: the writer's genuine originality and a stimulating, inspiring literary tradition. On the one hand, the writer's personal poetic proclivities undoubtedly play a prominent, paramount role in conceiving his or her aesthetic product. On the other hand, the writer's aesthetic product is also inspired and influenced by the literary tradition in which he or she is anchored as well as by works from other nationalities and languages.

Due to the cultural and social structure that existed prior to modern times, the role of tradition had been of singular importance. Often the traditional component overpowered the component of the artist's genuine originality. As a rule, the artist's originality, his or her unique personal aesthetic inclination, had not been as emphasized as in modern times. Indeed, in ancient arts what counted frequently was the artist's capacity to echo his or her predecessors' art. But, every rule has exceptions, and the history of the arts proves the validity of that rule. And the history of Hebrew poetry is not different. Thus, despite the apparent differences among the various literary periods through the long evolution of Hebrew literature, each of those literary periods obeyed the traditional decorum of poetic richness and rejected aesthetics of austerity. Whether some poets' personal proclivities were comfortable with that traditional decorum or not, it is hard to tell today. At any rate, Hebrew poetry over the last three millennia was not simple in structure and metaphor. Hebrew poetry had to wait three thousand years for David Fogel, the prince of aesthetics of austerity. Fogel was not the only one in his generation. No less a prince of aesthetics of austerity was his peer Abraham Ben-Itzhak (1883–1950), who wrote in the twenties and thirties. Fogel considered Ben-Itzhak his literary mentor, a source of aesthetic inspiration. For a variety of reasons, however, Fogel, and not Ben-Itzhak, is recognized as the father of aesthetics of austerity in modern Hebrew poetry, the one who blazed a new trail in Hebrew poetic modernism. The latter may be associated with the fact that despite Ben-Itzhak's prolific aesthetic crop, only twelve of his poems were published.

Contemporary Hebrew/Israeli Poetry

Who was David Fogel? Fogel was a "guest for the night" (see S. Y. Agnon's well-known novel of the same name), a rover, a wanderer. The idea of settling down was foreign to Fogel's personality and to the essence of his psychological mechanism.

Born in Russia in 1891, Fogel moved to Vienna in 1912, to Paris in 1926, and to the land of Israel in 1929. The eternal wanderer, the overnight guest who neither desires nor is able to strike roots in any one place, Fogel soon moved back to Vienna, sought his fortune in Berlin in 1931, and returned to Paris in 1932, by way of Poland. In 1944, Fogel died at the hands of the Nazis, as did six million of his brothers and sisters.

What made Fogel the prince of the aesthetics of austerity in modern Hebrew poetry? What initiated, inspired, and propelled that proclivity, which is so prominently displayed in his poetry? Two components interact in the "creation molecule": the writer's personal poetic disposition and the literary tradition which he or she has absorbed and internalized. Fogel's propensity for poetry is clear: he was fully aware of his aesthetic singularity—indeed, he proclaimed it proudly. The literary tradition that inspired and motivated him, it is evident that it was of a dual nature: Hebrew literature and German poetry. From Hebrew literature came the influences of two writers, whose influential "finger" can be detected in Fogel's poetry: the poet Abraham Ben-Itzhak and the novelist Uri Nissan Gnessin. Fogel's sequential images, his fluently flowing syntactical structures, the tinge of doom and gloom that pervades his works, the silent, subdued, undertoned rhetoric, somber atmosphere, tenderly formulated metaphors, dusky, dusty similes—all these display the influence of Ben-Itzhak's poetry on his peer/pupil Fogel.

The following lines are by Fogel:

> With gentle fingers
> The rain plays
> A somber, whispering song
> On the night's black organ.

Compare with the following verse. These lines are by Ben-Itzhak:

> A foreign, large night descended upon us
> And evening wind touched us and hummed
> like black violins.[3]

The similarity is striking here: the decadent, lament-like theme; the touching tone; the moving, doleful, gloomy metaphors; the gentleness in the flowing syntactical structures; the somber atmosphere; the mute, lamentational rhetoric; and the narrator's submissive, meek perspective. There is a hint of Anton Chekhov in these verses, a touch of deterioration, of decadence and decay, a silent sadness and the "sound" of gloom and doom; in other words, a suggestion of a mourning decline delivered through an understated, low-key rhetoric. Such is Fogel's aesthetics of austerity: a sequence of gentle images suffused with silken, delicate sights and sounds, melancholic rhetoric, austerely rendered patterns of syntax. In Fogel's rhetoric no trumpets sound; there is no sweepingly powerful Sturm und Drang or "sound and fury." Tender is the night: Fogel's rhetoric hums instead of drums; it possesses withering poetics instead of "sterling" aesthetics.

Yet, despite the simplicity of Fogel's poetry, it is not devoid of attractive intricacy. A fastidiously discriminating examination unveils in Fogel's work two principal layers: an upper layer (surface layer) that first addresses the reader and communicates on the most immediate

Mute and Tender

level, and a deeper, hidden layer, a cryptic layer that operates like an underlying current and may be unearthed through a meticulous process of close reading. The surface layer possesses fluent simplicity, modesty of structure, and austerity of theme and rhetoric; the deeper, cryptic layer has aesthetic sophistication and delicate intricacy. The overall meaning and appeal of the poem result from the dialogue between the two layers and derive from the reciprocal interaction between the surface and the cryptic layers.

Fogel found the novelist-storyteller Gnessin a significant source of inspiration. Indeed, no Hebrew writer during that literary period (twenties and thirties) was as intricate and sophisticated as Gnessin. He is the father of stream-of-consciousness in Hebrew literature, even though he was unable to read James Joyce, William Faulkner, Virginia Woolf, and other masters of stream-of-consciousness in Western literature, as they did not exist in Hebrew translation at the time. Most of Gnessin's stream-of-consciousness works reached aesthetic ripeness and maturity when such Western works were still in an embryonic state. In addition, Gnessin was both geographically and culturally remote from centers of Western literary creativity. He was active in Russia, but he apparently did not know enough English. He died in his early twenties. What attracted Fogel to Gnessin's aesthetics was the streamlined, flexible fluency of the language, the original metaphors, the misty, dusky, melancholic atmosphere, the expressive use of colors (notably yellow [used also by Knut Hamsun] and black to convey a sense of bleak, murky decay and somber despair), and the mood of decadence and degeneration.

Other non-Hebrew influences on Fogel's poetry range from the poet Rabindranath Tagore, the Indian Nobel Prize winner (1913), to the French symbolist school. He read them in German translation, however, because he did not know Bengali, Tagore's original language, and had only a modest command of French. Nevertheless, the atmosphere of neoromantic decadence, which prevailed in Vienna's literary circles at the dawn of the twentieth century, is quite noticeable in Fogel's poetry. Next to his intimate acquaintance with Hebrew literature, his familiarity with German literature—notably poetry—was most distinguished. One may assume that the simplicity of Russian acmeism (Anna Akhmatova and Osip Mandelstam, among others) also influenced Fogel's artistry. However, German poetry prior to expressionism provided the most significant non-Hebrew influence on Fogel, especially the works of Georg Trakl (actually Austrian), Georg Heym, Else Lasker-Schüler, and Rainer Maria Rilke. The suggestion of twilight and decadence, crumbling and decay, echo in Fogel's poetry.[4]

Nevertheless, all those influences neither eclipse nor cloud Fogel's evident originality. Writers are not deliberately influenced by other writers simply because they seek something missing in their own work. On the contrary, other writers influence a writer who finds in their works his or her own image. In Fogel's case, the adopted material is always carefully sifted and remolded to fit its new context. Fogel's borrowing was never less creative than his own work; the borrowed material gave rise to a new originality.[5]

Fogel also composed prose fiction: two erotically oriented novellas *(Facing the Sea* and *In the Sanatorium)*, a diary of significant literary quality, a fragmentary novel (in Yiddish) from his captivity in France during the Nazi occupation, and a sexually provocative novel (for the standards of the period) entitled *Married Life*.[6] Fogel's narrative is of an extremely impressionist nature and manifests the power struggle between the sexes, in which the woman takes the traditional literary role of the empowered *belle dame sans merci*.[7] As an artist of narrative, Fogel is an ardent disciple of August Strindberg, whose plays (notably the realistic ones) describe a blatantly bitter combat between the sexes, in which the man is tormented mentally by the woman. Fogel, as artist of narrative (no less than Fogel, the master of poetry), blazed a new trail in Hebrew literary modernism.

While Fogel composed his first poetic works of aesthetics of austerity, acmeism thrived in Russia and imagism emerged from the Western poetry of Ezra Pound, Amy Lowell, H.D., and others. In all those newborn literary trends, aesthetics of austerity dominated the ideological manifestos as well as the poetry. Indeed, the term "aesthetics of austerity" had not been coined, but its nature permeated and predominated in the composed verses. Its emergence toward the beginning of the twentieth century reflected historical changes occurring in society, economics, and culture. Political power transferred from unelected royalty to the masses. Economics was no longer controlled by arbitrary rulers but by vast social circles. It was a new world in which culture extricated itself from the limited radius of aristocracy and reached the masses. The arts mirrored all those changes and more. New movements, such as abstract painting, replaced traditional techniques in visual arts. A new artistic taste emerged, and it was time for aesthetics of austerity to speak out.

The aesthetics of austerity turned its back on poetics that fit only those who led lives of plenty. Aristocracy shrank at the start of the new era. The masses expressed themselves and delivered their message for the first time. And the aesthetics of austerity, with its simplicity that denied aristocratic aesthetics, addressed the masses. In this respect, Russian acmeism and Western imagism offered for the first time simple, unpretentious poetry: poetry in blue jeans instead of tuxedos. Furthermore, modern art no longer desired only to mirror or interpret reality; it now desired also to take part in creating reality, in molding and sculpting reality.

Fogel, however, was not a social revolutionary; he was the epitome of an individual talent who is divorced from social circles and processes. Fogel was always zealous for of his privacy and allowed no one to invade his secluded realms. And yet, on an aesthetic level, Fogel was a citizen of the aesthetic environment in which he lived. While he remained alienated from social and political processes that yielded a new literary trend, he was not alienated from that trend it-self. Although some Hebrew critics welcomed Fogel's aesthetics of austerity (including the celebrated novelist and literary ideologist Yosef Chaim Brenner), others made no attempt to conceal their rejection of Fogel's aesthetics. Chaim Nachman Bialik, the leading figure of modern Hebrew poetry and a highly influential literary figure, detested Fogel's aesthetics, and Bialik was not the only one.

Perhaps it was only a matter of aesthetic taste on Bialik's part, perhaps there was more. Perhaps Bialik felt about Fogel the way an old patriarch feels about a young successor who threatens to take over his territory and to dislodge him from the position of power (as effectively discussed by Freud in *Totem and Taboo*). After all, literature evolves when writers rebel against the literary traditions of past generations. Bialik's opposition to Fogel's aesthetics of austerity, however, stymied Fogel's ability to get the poetic acceptance that he undoubtedly deserved. Bialik, the great master of "aristocratic"—almost prophetic—trends in poetry, a poet of glamorous richness and stupendous complexity, was a rival of such august, mighty magnitude that he cast a shadow on Fogel's poetry and diminished its role in the development of modern Hebrew poetry. Perhaps "suspended" would be more appropriate than "diminished." During the fifties, a new literary generation emerged, rediscovered Fogel's poetry, and paid him homage. Among them was Nathan Zach, the faithful disciple who redeemed Fogel's poetry from the obscurity to which Bialik—and later Shlonsky and Alterman—had consigned it.

Although Zach does not embrace wholeheartedly Fogel's poetic credo, he does seem to have internalized the aesthetic lesson that Fogel bequeathed to modern Hebrew poetry. Nathan Zach was born in Germany in 1930. He immigrated to the land of Israel in 1935 and spent many years in England, where he wrote his doctoral dissertation on the imagist poets. Nowadays, together with the late Yehuda Amichai, he is considered the most celebrated figure in contemporary

Hebrew/Israeli poetry. He is an emeritus professor of literature at Haifa University. Like Fogel, Zach was exposed to German poetry of the early twentieth century, yet Zach found his most natural element, the icon of his poetic credo, in imagism.

Zach's enthusiasm for aesthetics of austerity cannot, however, be separated from his harsh attack on the poetry of Nathan Alterman. Zach's preference for Fogel over Alterman not only reflects his own poetic proclivities, his own "aesthetic cup of tea," it also obeys a literary-historical rule: a new literary generation revolts against the "giants" of the previous generation by advocating the writers whom the previous generation largely ignored, denied, and rejected. In Zach's case, the previous generation considered Alterman a giant who must be exiled from a position of poetic power. Fogel, on the contrary, was invited to return from the aesthetic exile to which he was doomed by Bialik.

Why did Alterman's poetry elicit so much opposition from Zach? Alterman is known for his exceedingly metaphorical language, which is highly flowery, innovative and daring; for his colorful and rich fictional world; for his intricate symbolic themes and his strict yet sweeping metrical, rhythmical rhyme patterns. Zach objected mainly to the intensely figurative nature of Alterman's poetry and its rhymed and precisely measured rhythmical features.[8] Zach does not deny Alterman's poetic talent, but he seeks to replace Alterman's "sterling sublimity" with humble simplicity, to restrain his emotionality, and to replace his marchlike meter with one that is flexible, tranquil, and quietly, fluently flowing. Perhaps Zach's is a typical revolt against a dominant ancestor, a revolt that always mixes rejection with adoration. But it is principally a clash between two contradictory schools of aesthetics.

Contemporary Israeli poetry has not been the same since the publication of Zach's poems and his harshly critical essay "Meditations on Alterman's Poetry." One of the major targets is Alterman's metrical system. Zach claims that Alterman's rhythmical patterns, which are extremely precise and pedantically orchestrated, create an effect which is stiff, rigid, and forced, hopelessly at odds with the content, and consequently undermines the thematic fabric of the poem as well as its leading ideas. Zach also criticizes Alterman's sentimentality, affected attitude toward reality, and his too-lofty metaphorical patterns.[9] Thus, it is not surprising that Zach demonstrates a strong attraction to the imagist movement in poetry, a movement that engraved on its ideological banner the demand for composing "in sequence of the musical verse, not in sequence of a metronome."[10] The literary historian is the one to decide whether Zach's opposition to Alterman's poetry first derived from his acquaintance with the imagist school, or whether an intuitive rejection of Alterman's led him to look for a theoretical support. However, Zach's recoil from Alterman's overblown symbolism and metrical precision reflects the major ideals of the imagist movement: "clarity, exactness or concreteness of detail," "economy of language," and rejection of "the flabby, abstract language and structure" of symbolist poetry.[11]

To the imagist poets, the supreme source of poetic evil was the symbolist poets' verbal congestion of overflowing metaphors and their devotion to tempestuous rhythm. As Ford Madox Ford put it, "I desired to see English become at once more colloquial and more exact, verse more fluid and more exacting of its practitioners."[12] And when Zach opened his well-known poem "The Correct Poem" with the words "When the sentiment fades, the correct poem speaks," he definitely made a declaration of allegiance to imagist poetry. Hence, Zach's obstinate resistance to Alterman's poetics, on the one hand, and his ardently enthusiastic acceptance of the imagist poetics, on the other, are two sides of the same aesthetic coin. Indeed, not only Ezra Pound and his imagist poet disciples influenced Zach's poetic views but also poets like T. S. Eliot, e. e. cummings, Wallace Stevens, and William Carlos Williams—poets who were themselves influenced by the imagists.[13] For example, in Zach's poetry we see the influence of cummings's puns, paradoxes, and inversions; Stevens's comic devices, syntactical patterns, and intellectualism; and Williams's concrete nature. In addition, Zach is greatly impressed by Eliot's sharp-witted irony, his penetrating, piercing intellect, and the "obscure coherence" of composition, all of which serve as efficient arms against the sentimentality of Victorian poetry. In fact, Zach's revolt against Alterman has echoes of Eliot's revolt against Tennyson.[14] Indeed, Zach's poetry, in its very essence, is a poetry of "desentimentalization," of opposition to overloaded expression, of rebellion against the direct statement of feeling. Correspondingly, in his eternal battle against sentimental congestion in his poetry, Zach mobilizes very effective ammunition: irony. When irony is enlisted, sentiment is disarmed.

A principal aim of Zach's poetry is to exile the archenemy of poetry—sloppy sentiment. Control emotion, dim emotion, dam emotion, mute emotion, restrain emotion: this could be the principal slogan of Zach's *ars poetica*. Emotion is not canceled in Zach's poetry; it is concealed. To meet this challenge, Zach mobilizes several literary techniques, in addition to those borrowed from his influential aesthetic ancestors. Expectations are set up and demolished. Confusing syntax, rhetorical gaps, puzzling rhyme systems, enigmatic statements—these are some of Zach's poetic ammunition against the sentimental effect. All of these compel the reader to mobilize and utilize intellectual, rational faculties upon decoding and cracking the poem's enigmatic texture. And intellectualism and rationalism force the reader to distance him- or herself from the text. Such a distance avoids identification, and a lack of identification silences sentimentality. Again, it is not sentiment that Zach objects to but sentimentality. In his essay "A Note on Poetry," William Carlos Williams states that the poet's function is "to lift, by use of his imagination and the language he hears, the material conditions and appearances of this

The Witty Touch of Simplicity

environment to the sphere of the intelligence."[15] Zach's poetry shows that he is a faithful believer in this view. He uses the process of intellectualization as a rhetorical filter through which identification with the text is dammed and consequently sentiment is sifted. Under these circumstances, Zach's wish is fulfilled: sentiment fades and what he calls the "correct poem" speaks. Robert Pack, in his thorough study of Wallace Stevens's poetry, emphasizes that "the irony, the humor, the self-satire are means by which Stevens' comic imagination keeps the proper distance from things."[16] Zach accomplishes the same goal by using irony as well as sarcastic humor, shattered structures, and high rhetoric—all of which, as stressed above, hush and mute sentimentality. And it is also this goal that has goaded Zach to adopt the techniques of "nonsense."[17]

Many of Zach's poems demonstrate an affinity to nonsense poetry: they are based on a confusing cluster of phrases that seem to be hopelessly disconnected from each other. No controlling logic is at first apparent, and the (fictional) words of the poem seem puzzling and meaningless. For instance, in his poem "A burning heat night," he writes: "a town has burst into song—if it has not done it yet. / A tourist in a hotel. / A pregnant woman / A senior officer."[18] But Zach's poetry deviates from the fundamental nature of nonsense poetry. Nonsense poetry is based upon "a carefully limited world, controlled and directed by reason, a construction subject to its own laws."[19] In contrast, Zach's enigmatic texture does not present an isolated alien world that operates according to logic and laws of its own but is anchored in the very heart of our world. Like Chagall's painting, which violates the common order of reality, Zach's enigmatic poems breach logical and realistic structures for one purpose: exposing the heart of the truth of that reality.

The confusing features of many of Zach's enigmatic poems should not deceive us; they don't wish to evict the readers from their own reality but to reacquaint them with their reality. One should read those poems as one reads a metaphor: the "chaotic" verbal surface should function not as a stumbling block but as a set of directions that lead to the hidden meaning. The use of distorted logic and odd combinations is not a flashy, attention-getting sleight-of-hand but part of the poet's conscious process of intellectualization that aims at evoking emotion while avoiding sentimentality. Zach's poetry is not nonsense poetry but poetry that adopts nonsense techniques for one goal: to restrain sentiment and permit the "correct poem" to speak.[20]

Thus, perhaps the most significant aesthetic tool enlisted by Zach in his "mutiny" against sentimentality is intellectuality. Zach bestows upon his poetry such a clear intellectual touch that the reader reacts on an intellectual level while eschewing any possible sentimental reaction. Before being allowed to feel Zach's poetry, the reader is forced to intellectualize it. And intellect is the archenemy of sentiment. In this respect, Zach is more an admirer of Fogel than his disciple; the intellectual qualities and the irony which are such a natural part of Zach's poetry are alien to Fogel's poetics. Nevertheless, despite the fact that the two "speak different poetic languages," they share the same ideological "dictionary." Both oppose poetic gaudiness and both produce aesthetics of austerity.

Thus, the "poetic gospel" of aesthetics of austerity may justly be considered an Archimedean launching point, a springboard from which contemporary Hebrew/Israeli poetry embarked on its new aesthetic path. Or to put it differently, aesthetics of austerity served as an artistic recipe for contemporary Hebrew/Israeli poetry: its seeds planted and rooted in the fifties and its fruits and flowers budded and blossomed to the fullest in the sixties. Hence, Nathan Zach's and David Fogel's ars poetica define the agenda and the boundaries of contemporary Hebrew/Israeli poetry, its prevailing contours as well as its meridians and latitudes.

Contemporary Hebrew/Israeli poetry has never been enslaved to those aesthetic outlines or caged in their confines. In this respect, one can describe Fogel's and Zach's joint poetic platform as a musical score which enables the conductor and the performers to play it while interpreting its musical notes and instructions according to their own artistic inclinations. The principles dictated to contemporary Hebrew/Israeli poetry by Fogel's and Zach's aesthetic legacy have been by and large preserved. Contemporary Hebrew/Israeli poetry refrains from cryptically complex symbolism; from thunderlike rhetoric; from cultivating ideas that are remote from daily life; and from fastidiously measured patterns of rhythm, meter, and rhyme. Those are certainly generalizations, but whatever exceptions exist do not vitiate the validity of the generalization. On the contrary, the exceptions fertilize and vitalize the generalization and bestow upon it a vivacious flexibility that avoids undesirable rigidity. Hence, beyond the aesthetic boundaries set by Fogel and Zach, as well as by Amichai, Avidan, and the *Likrat* literary group, contemporary Hebrew/Israeli poetry displays and invites different poetic options and numerous interpretations of its principal poetic platform.

Three Poems by Asher Reich

The poetry of Asher Reich, one of the most appealing voices in the choir of contemporary Hebrew/Israeli poetry, provides an excellent example of the most dramatic, extreme, and daring interpretations of that genre. The aesthetic essence of Reich's poetry, its fundamental poetic DNA, can aptly be described as vivid, vibrant, and vitally passionate expressionism. His powerful expressionism is formed through the use of colorful, sensual metaphors, dramatic erotic themes, and vivid images. The language is saturated with remarkably complex semantic fields in which biblical and postbiblical (Mishnaic/Talmudic) allusions are dexterously interlaced.

The lyrical speaker in a typical Reich poem conveys the text and orchestrates the dialogue between the text and the reader (the text meets the reader's emotional mechanism and intellectual faculties, and the reader responds both emotionally and intellectually). However, the speaker carefully and skillfully curbs his or her own reaction to the reality portrayed in the poem, avoiding excessive sentimentality, while at the same time maintaining his or her passion and attitude like a scorching flame. That flamelike quality is evident in poems that deal with erotic tendencies, sensuality, and stormy sexuality. The expressionist, passionate, fervent nature of Reich's lyrical speaker is a dominant, dramatic characteristic of his poetic portrait. Other characteristics by which Reich's poetry stretches the boundaries of aesthetics of austerity (the aesthetic context of contemporary Hebrew/Israeli poetry in which he is deeply anchored) include rich metaphorical textures; expressionism founded upon fervid devotion to the poem's theme and message while using a rapturous tone; gushing emotions that are metaphorically reflected through encompassing series of colorful, picturesque images; and tempestuous sensuality and frank, bold, sexuality.

Reich's poetic portrait seems to challenge the restrained aspects of aesthetics of austerity but he exceeds them in a way that cleverly avoids overstepping their basic poetic formulas and models. More-over, the intimate, confessional, engaging tone of the lyrical speaker effectively softens and restrains the poem's tempestuousness and helps keep it within the purviews of aesthetics of austerity. Corre-spondingly, Reich's poetry plays a prominent role in the arena of contemporary Hebrew/Israeli poetry. It contributes to its compre-hensive character a remarkably colorful, engaging tone as well of powerful, bountiful, captivating and dramatic qualities. Thus, Reich's poetry bestows passionate, vivacious plenty upon Hebrew/Is-raeli poetry, while simultaneously paying homage to its predecessors from the fifties, those who preached aesthetics of austerity.

An analysis of Reich's poem "An Aerial Photograph" ("*Tzilum Avi-ri*") will show how he cogently displays these qualities.[21] The discus-sion will reveal the mechanism that harnesses the aesthetic aspects and qualities to the poem's philosophical agenda and ideological message. It will also show the clever, intricate, mosaic-like interac-tion among the poem's various strata. While each of them has a sep-arate, independent function, their fusion in one aesthetic piece pro-duces a multilayered, synchronic orchestration.

An Aerial Photograph

And suddenly gun fire was aiming at me in the field
And I knew it was aiming at me from the north.
Exhausted, I collapsed on the soil from which I came
And those skies came upon me dreadfully
Broken sounds broken sounds pierced in me a hollow—

Despite its remarkably compact character, the poem possesses a dense cluster of aesthetic characteristics that are typical of Reich's poetic temperament. The language displays a colorful variety, as well as rich, plentiful, abundant metaphors and subtle linguistic intricacy. The dense alliterative "textual tissues" (which are regrettably lost in the English translation) conceive and yield a vital, vivid vocalism. Despite its brevity, the poem is densely populated by literary and biblical allusions, which contribute to the poem's aesthetic complexity while imbuing the message with a universal application.

The lyrical speaker confesses to a haunting, personal distress. He expresses his complaint in striking, sensual language. While the poem clearly rests on solid and sound realistic foundations, its "realistic fabric" operates as an "agent" of a different reality, one of both symbolic and universal characteristics. While the poem portrays personal experiences associated with a contemporary reality, it equally echoes experiences suggesting fantastic, distant, misty, legendary aspects of reality. The poem prudently, dexterously eschews sentimentality by enlisting a dense, bounteous dose of irony.

The poem's ironic tenor brings to mind the spirit of *Kohelet* (Ecclesiastes): a tolerant acceptance of reality, for all its distress and oppressiveness, with no expectations of deliverance. Thus, the self-ironical narrator sadly and realistically accepts the optimistic prophecy of Isaiah *"vehaya he'akov lemishor"* ("and the rugged shall become plain," Isaiah 40:4).[22] The optimistic spirit is fated to be frustrated. To decipher the poem and discover its ideas and messages, we must trace the crowded, overflowing sequence of allusions that make up its texture, cracking the aesthetic code encrypted in those allusions.

The poem begins with a complex cluster of allusions associated with different semantic fields and historical circumstances: "And suddenly gun fire was aiming [*niftecha*, 'opened, broke out'] at me in the field [*basadeh*]." This allusion is socially and culturally oriented, referring as it does to contemporary Israeli circumstances in the battlefield. That the gun fire was shot "in the field" further reinforces the military frame of reference.

36

The next line, "And I knew it was aiming at me from the north," contains a biblical allusion: *"Mitzafon tipatach hara'ah"* ("From the north shall calamity break out," Jeremiah 1:14). Reich introduces the concept of a calamity (deadly gun fire) with nearly the same wording: but his version is even clearer and more powerful. The word "field" in the first line, while being associated with deadly circumstances, may be yet another biblical allusion, the slaying of Abel by his jealous older brother, Cain: "And when they were in the field, Cain set upon his brother Abel and killed him" (Genesis 4:8).

Thus, the poem's opening lines yield a semantically complex intersection where three allusions meet and interact. Two of them are enlisted from the Bible; the third is from contemporary Israel. Each of these relates to a deadly event (all three take place *basadeh*/in the field), and the cumulative effect of the three combines Israel's present with Israel's distant past to evoke a sense of death and destruction.

The poem's third line is just as rich in allusions: "Exhausted, I collapsed on the soil from which I came." The collapse on the soil, the very earth and dust from which the narrator (like all his fellow human beings) came, naturally echoes the well-known biblical passage: "For dust you are, and to dust you shall return" (Genesis 3:20). Reich's poem uses the same word that the Bible uses for soil/earth/dust, *aphar,* lending further validity to the biblical connection. Since the biblical passage is associated with human loss of immortality (due to the Fall, the first human iniquity), it conveys a grim message, in accord with the general drift of the poem.

The same tone prevails in the poem all the way to the last word, "hollow" *("khalal").* In Hebrew *khalal* means not only void or emptiness but also a dead person (notably a person killed in war), and thus here seems to echo another Bible verse: "If someone is found slain *[khalal]* . . . in the field" (Deuteronomy 21:1). Here again the biblical allusion evokes the idea of finality, doom, and death. The repetition of the word "field" in this biblical allusion and in the previous one

(Cain kills Abel in the field; gunfire is aimed at the narrator in the field) further underscores the intricate set of allusions in the text.

The strong hint of death that haunts the poem and its narrator gains further prominence at the conclusion of the poem: "Broken sounds, broken sounds . . ." *("shevarim, shevarim").* This expression from the Jewish prayer book is used to evoke and echo the broken sounds produced by the blowing of the horn (shofar) during Yom Kippur, the day of atonement (as well as during Rosh Hashana, the Jewish New Year). Those broken sounds *(shevarim)* announcing the end of the Jewish holiest day, symbolize the human attempt to pierce the skies (the word "pierced" in the poem is associated with the broken sounds) in order to reach to heaven and to earn God's forgiveness, compassion, and blessing. In fact, next to "broken sounds" *(shevarim),* the Jewish prayer book (in Yom Kippur section) includes one more instruction on how to blow the shofar: *teru'ah* (a loud blast). However, the poem deliberately omits that instruction for the shofar blower, keeping only *shevarim* (broken sounds), which relates to something defective, blemished, fractured, shattered, crushed, or ruptured. The poem omits the allusion to the complete, continuous sound of the shofar but retains the allusion to the broken sound. That omission is neither arbitrary nor random: it demonstrates a preference for the broken sound over the complete sound. While the complete sound is at odds with the poem's murky message of gloom and doom, the broken sound aptly reflects the poem's somber, morbid, deadly message. Moreover, the repetition of the same word/s ("broken sounds, broken sounds") is typical of biblical laments, for instance, David's lament for his slain, rebellious son, Absalom: "My son Absalom, Absalom my son, my son" (2 Samuel 9:1). Thus, the poem further reinforces the somber atmosphere, associated with death, by echoing the Bible's typical lament rhetoric. The poem displays artistic sophistication in its effective use of allusions, which deliver its somber and pessimistic message.[23]

As Yom Kippur may justly be compared with doomsday (since on Yom Kippur God judges all people and sentences them to either life or death), alluding to Yom Kippur in the poem further reinforces the biblical allusions (as well as the allusion to contemporary Israeli wars), all conferring on the poem a sense of doom and death. The skies which are expected to open during the ending of Yom Kippur (due to the piercing broken sounds produced by the horn) are portrayed in the poem as an overwhelming, gigantic entity that suffocates the narrator, collapsing on his crushed body: "And those skies came upon me dreadfully." The unexpected nature of the image evokes sharp irony here (the skies are expected to open compassionately for the narrator, not shatter him under their overwhelmingly heavy weight). This reinforces the general tone of the poem as well as enhances its intricate network of allusions. Moreover, the portrayal of the skies coming dreadfully upon the shattered narrator suggests sexual aggressiveness, even a vulgar, violent rape. This sense is heightened by the use of the verb "to come" in "came upon me" *("ba'u alay"),* which is commonly used in the Bible to describe sexual intercourse between a male and female (for instance, "and he came to her and she conceived by him," Genesis 38:16). Thus, compounding a violent assault by the skies against the tormented narrator with sexual aggressiveness bestows upon the apocalyptic scene a sense of unbridled brutality. The fact that death and sexuality were often intermingled in seventeenth-century English metaphysical poetry further underscores the poem's apocalyptic message of tragic mortality, deadly gloom, and violent, pugnacious sexuality.

Thus, the poem gains at least part of its intriguing intricacy by presenting the theme of death and violent, belligerent mortality with a cluster of complex allusions (most of them biblical) that introduce death from a variety of perspectives: death in the contemporary Israeli battlefield, the death of Abel in the field, the dead man found in the field, the deadly calamity approaching from the north, the

A Hounding Day of Doom

penalty of death because of original sin that makes humans return to the soil from which they came, the grim possibility of a deadly verdict on Yom Kippur, death insinuated by echoes of biblical rhetoric of lament, and death associated with suffocating, aggressive sexuality, even a violent rape that holds deadly connotations. This singular complexity, which condenses numerous perspectives in five short lines, is softened by the viewpoint of a lyrical speaker, who presents his agonizing message in the compelling, compassionately personal fashion of a confession.

Concluding this short poem on such a forceful note epitomizes the unique poetic genius of Asher Reich. It demonstrates his ability to combine complexity, bold sexuality, morbidity, subtle intricacy, and assertive directness in the texture of one slim poem, a touching appeal for comfort and compassion. In this respect, Reich's poetry offers the most daring and dramatic interpretation of aesthetics of austerity. It seems to produce a small, yet remarkable miracle: fire and ice, flame and frost, inextricably intertwined.

An analysis of two more poems will show how Reich dictates and shapes a poem with themes, motifs, and poetic temperament. The deliberate choice of two poems that are quite different from each other provides an opportunity to probe and comprehend the larger scope of Reich's poetics, its subtle nuances and diversity, and its overall intriguing complexity. The first poem's title, "An Aerial Photograph," locates the narrator in a remote, distant point of view, one that observes the poem's emotional chronicles from high above. That rhetorical distance bestows upon the reader a far-away perspective that keeps him or her from being swept away or flooded by the poem's emotions. This way, aesthetically "befouled" sentimentality is silenced, and the poem meets success upon evoking passionate emotionality. That prudently "sculpted" balance between plus and minus calls for ardent admiration.

The second poem is "Power Break" *("Hafsakat Khashmal").*

Hafsakat Khashmal/Power [Electricity] Break

Behold the candle: there, over its slowly transforming body
    in my room,
A soundless vision of a mute beauty is erecting
Alone, an upright safeguard, deep down into the dead of
    the night
It is blazing a zone, unearthing a space, for myself only.

If only could I cope, wrestle with the towering darkness until
    it turns soundless
I shall wait here. I shall stay still until seeing the sounds of
    the candle.

A worm of light is swimming slowly in the rustling darkness.
Tonight, like a fisherman I have set a snare of patience
Aiming at those who are walking.

A myrtle puddle is gleaming, glowing in the morning
Like a socket in the wall, which surely shall be penetrated
By the sun's thread: the light of our souls.

Even at first blush, an educated reader can discern a cluster of biblical allusions strewn along the poem's textual continuum. The fact that an intricately woven network of such allusions is "anchored" in the poem, and the allusions are carefully and strategically distributed, attests to the poem's intricate artistry. Their complex concentration adds intensity and resonance to the universal message that the poem conveys, a timeless, boundless message that transcends all cultural differences.

The first word of the poem, "behold," is an easily recognized biblical allusion to prophecy. For instance, God uses the same word—behold *(habet)*—when God promises Abraham that his offspring will be as numerous as the stars in the skies: "Behold the skies and count the stars, if you are able to count them; such shall be your [countless] offspring" (Genesis 15:5). The phrase that opens (in the original Hebrew text) the second line of the first stanza carries similar biblical connotations of prophecy: *kam mare'h* (a scene, or view, is arising, erecting). For instance, in the famous poetic—and metaphorical—prophecy by the prophet Ezekiel, commonly called "the vision of the dry bones," the prophet employs the word *mare'h* to denote a vision, a prophecy: "And the presence of God of Israel appeared there, like the vision *[mare'h]* that I had seen in the valley" (Ezekiel 8:4). The story of the burning bush in Numbers 8:4 also uses the word *mare'h* to tell of divine prophecy: "like the vision *[mare'h]* that God has shown Moses in the desert."

The second stanza of the poem is also rich in biblical allusions that meet, cross, and interact:

> If only could I cope, wrestle with the towering darkness until
> it turns soundless
> I shall wait here. I shall stay still until seeing the sounds of
> the candle.

The scene involving human wrestling in the darkness, on the one hand, and waiting for the darkness to fade away, on the other, echoes Jacob wrestling in the darkness with the celestial messenger until darkness fades away and dawn breaks (Genesis 32:24). The metaphorical expression—the darkness that will turn soundless, that is, will turn into light as dawn breaks—brings to mind a similar biblical scene, although of a "reverse" nature. What makes that biblical allusion valid is the fact that in both the alluding text (the poem) and the alluded text (the biblical scene under consideration), the same verb/root is used to produce a pattern of alliteration: *yidom* (turns soundless), in the poem, *va-yidom* in the Bible: "*Va-yidom* [stood still, or kept silent] the sun, and the moon halted" (Joshua 10: 13). And later in the same stanza: "*loh amush*" ("I'll stand still"). That biblical allusion embedded in the poem gains further validity since both texts involve a situation that demands coping with difficulty. In both texts, a dramatic determination is applied. In the poem there is a desire to tussle with the power of nature (darkness turns into light); in the biblical text, there is a desire to control nature (Joshua's command that the sun halt until the Israelites meet victory in the battlefield, which soon turns into reality).

Another biblical allusion in the second stanza leads the reader to the powerful spectacle of Moses descending from Mount Sinai, holding the two tablets upon which the Ten Commandments are engraved, while the mountain is shrouded in a cloud of thick smoke. A loud, roaring thunder is heard and bright, radiating lightning flickers. The biblical narrator reports the Israelites' response to that stupendous, majestic event in a puzzling, enigmatic fashion: "And all the people are seeing the sounds . . ." (Exodus 20:15). This enigmatic expression, which is at odds with empirical reality (one cannot see sounds, only hear them), is neither random nor arbitrary. The unusual formulation is intentionally designed to reflect the mysterious splendor of the event, its out-of-this-world nature: God Himself materializes on the sacred mountain in the form of smoky cloud, thunder, and lightning. It is hard to miss that biblical allusion in the second stanza: "I shall stay still until seeing the sounds of the candle." In the poem, the words "stay still" echo the Israelites' stillness during the momentous event on Mount Sinai, while the reference to the candle alludes to God's lightning. Together they underscore the connection. This biblical allusion bestows upon the poem a mysterious, eerie quality, which accords well with both the atmosphere and the meaning the poem is designed to convey.

The poem's narrator evokes another biblical allusion when he declares, "I shall stay still" *("loh amush").* Exodus 13:22 also uses the verb *amush* (although conjugated slightly differently): "The pillar of cloud by day and the pillar of fire by night shall stay still *[loh yamish]* from before the people." That biblical allusion is also associated with a "pillar of fire"—the flaming candle, one of the most prominent themes in the poem. The fact that this biblical allusion relates to both pillars, of cloud and of fire, connects it to the previous one, the appearance of fire before the Israelites when they receive the Ten Commandments and the laws of the Torah. Thus, the alluding mechanism is founded on interaction between the poem's alluding text and the biblical alluded text. The alluded biblical texts, which are interwoven in the poem, conduct a "dialogue" among themselves on top of the one they conduct with the poem's alluding text.

The extensive embroidery of biblical allusions proves even more complex when the reader discovers and identifies another biblical allusion. The narrator metaphorically compares himself to a fisherman who sets a snare of patience to serve "those who are walking [in darkness]," until they see "a myrtle puddle [that] is gleaming, glowing in the morning [a source of light]." The line echoes the following biblical passage: "The people who are walking in the darkness have seen a brilliant light" (Isaiah 9:1).

This elaborate mosaic of biblical metaphors and allusions is indeed formidable, but it is not merely an aesthetic feat. It also conveys a universal message and prevailing philosophical proclivities, a singular historical breadth and depth, a celebrated atmosphere and a spectacular impact. When there is a confluence of form and theme with imagery and ideas, the text of the poem takes on an exquisite aesthetic tapestry. But when these also advance the poem's theme, the aesthetic tapestry of biblical allusions becomes even more worthy.

At this stage of the analysis the reader is equipped with sufficient information to move to the next stage of the interpretation, ready to unearth more hidden structures and patterns in the poem's textual fabric. First, however, it is important to note that the poem contains aesthetics and ideology characteristic of metaphysical poetry (that of John Donne, Andrew Marvell, George Herbert, and others from seventeenth-century England).[24] For example, the poem carries a strong hint of sexuality (the erect candle, the myrtle puddle, the worm of light that moves slowly in the darkness, the "socket in the wall in which surely shall be penetrated / The sun's thread," the marriage between the light and the soul) intermingled with religious experiences (consisting of numerous biblical allusions, most of them associated with prophetic visions as well as with God's formidably majestic appearance). The mystical aspects (the mute beauty erected in the dark, the rustling darkness, the patient yet anxious waiting for an epiphany) all express the narrator's inclination toward introspection and the mystery of love and death, God and humanity. All of the above are in cogent congruence with English metaphysical poetry of the seventeenth century.

The first stanza makes use of some aesthetic aspects of metaphysical poetry, while retaining its own unique character. The narrator seems fascinated by the erect candle as its "slowly transforming body" conjures up a vision of muted beauty and blazes a zone for the narrator alone. The enchanting, mysterious atmosphere informing this stanza stems from the mystic nocturnal scene in which an erotic, phallic candle rises in the dead of night, while the spellbound narrator responds to the candle with a biblical allusion to a prophetic vision: "Behold." In the second line, "mute beauty" instead of "unseen beauty" is an image reminiscent of metaphysical poetry whereby two elements at odds with the logic of empirical reality are conjoined. The metaphorical oxymoron enhances and reinforces the stanza's mysterious quality and its nocturnal atmosphere.

The second stanza further develops the main theme of the previous stanza, creating more mystery, paradox, and religious overtones, all strongly redolent of metaphysical poetry. The narrator wishes he possessed the strength to cope and wrestle with the towering darkness "until it turns soundless." The outcome of that struggle with the towering darkness will allow the narrator to see "the sounds of the candle." This paradoxical expression, as explained earlier, alludes to the majestic, lordly spectacle of God appearing on Mount Sinai as the Israelites receive the Ten Commandments from Moses and "the people see the sounds." The strong erotic connotations of the second stanza are also typical of metaphysical poetry. The narrator's desire to cope and wrestle with the "towering darkness" echoes the previous stanza's theme with its erect candle, which is metaphorically compared to an upright (erect) safeguard.

One notices a causal connection between the two stanzas, as the second one naturally evolves from the first. The subtle sexuality of the first two stanzas gathers momentum in the third stanza. The narrator follows the erotic coiling and winding of the phallic "worm of light" while it is "swimming slowly in the rustling darkness" (the latter is a metonym for the female intimate parts). The religious connotations in the poem's first two stanzas (also associated with biblical prophecy, divine visions, and sublime manifestations of the divine) echo vigorously in the third stanza as well. The narrator portrays himself metaphorically as a fisherman who "set a snare of patience," in order to attract "those who are walking," again, as in Isaiah 16:1: "The people who are walking in the darkness have seen a brilliant light." In the previous stanza the biblical allusion was to the appearance of God on Mount Sinai, thus conferring upon the narrator (who stays still, like the people of Israel on that occasion) a majestic role, equating him with the ancient Israelites who were granted the Godly privilege of witnessing such an awesome event. However, in the third stanza, the narrator's already elevated role seems to become even loftier. He appears like the chosen *mevasser* [25] (a divine guide or harbinger who proclaims God's words and shows the way to the entire nation, as in Isaiah 41:27: "And again I [God] send a herald /harbinger [*mevasser*] to Jerusalem"). Thus, the narrator in the third stanza is the one who is directly associated with the role of a Godly herald, who shall lead "those who are walking in the darkness" to see a bright, celestial light. While in the second stanza, the narrator is passively associated with a Godly epiphany, his divine role is upgraded in the third stanza to an active one: a Godly herald, *mevasser*, who blazes a trail for the people walking in the darkness, heading for a celestial light. This progressive, dynamic motion is echoed in the poem's parallel track, the erotic one. While in the first stanza, the erotic candle is relatively passive (only its body is "slowly transforming"), in the third stanza, the erotic candle's presence becomes more active as it is metaphorically compared with "a worm of light . . . swimming slowly in the rustling darkness."

The poem, then, presents two parallel tracks, which develop and evolve simultaneously: the divine track and the erotic track. Both tracks interact, echoing and reflecting each other. This two-track process reaches its culmination in the poem's fourth and last stanza where both tracks (the erotic one and the Godly one) unite again, following the ideological practice of metaphysical poetry. The first line of the fourth stanza, "A myrtle puddle is gleaming, glowing in the morning," is the fruition of the prophetic, biblical allusion from Isaiah that ended the previous stanza ("The people who are walking in the darkness will see a bright light"). This line has subtle sexual connotations as well as prophetic biblical ones. Myrtle is traditionally associated with sexuality, notably as its liquid characteristics are found after the night (see, for instance, Song of Songs 5:5: "I rose to let in by beloved . . . my hands dripping myrtle"). In the last stanza, the two separate strains—erotic and religious—meet and interact, producing a sublime union, one that echoes metaphysical poetry. The last two lines of the poem mirror the theme: "Like a socket in the wall, which surely shall be penetrated / By the sun's thread: the light of our souls." The penetration of the "socket in the wall" by "the sun's thread" is clearly a metaphor for sexual intercourse. On the other hand, the "gleaming, glowing" light of the myrtle puddle suggests an analogy with the biblical allusion in the third stanza to "a bright light." That biblical allusion can be further elaborated. First, the last stanza relates to a socket that is also a source of light. Second, the last stanza ends with the metaphorical phrase "the light of our souls." These two references to light underscore the analogy between the "gleaming, glowing" light of the myrtle puddle and "bright light" in Isaiah. In the last stanza, the two strains (sexuality and religious spirituality) are unified with the concluding phrase, "the light of our souls." The expression has clear connotations of religious spirituality; the enlightened, illuminated soul is a familiar concept in religious thinking. But it also evokes a literary allusion to concealed sexuality. One need only recall the opening line of Vladimir Nabokov's *Lolita,* "Lolita, light of my life, fire of my loins," to appreciate the spiritually/sexually oriented words "light of our souls." This last phrase captures in a nutshell the stanza's main theme, which unites the poem's two separate strains of religious spirituality and a sweeping celebration of sexuality.

The same tendency can be further detected in another oxymoron. On the one hand, the socket ("Like a socket in the wall") is a source of electricity and light, which joins the poem's numerous references to a celestial light, perhaps even a Messianic light, with unmistakable religious connotations. On the other hand, the socket is also a symbol of female sexuality, notably in the last stanza, where it is "penetrated" by a phallic "sun's thread" (the sun being another source of light, associated with the poem's celestial light). Indeed, it may reflect the Jewish metaphorical portrayal of sexual intercourse on a spiritual basis between God (the male source of light) and the Sabbath (female). The poem presents a powerful sense of a sublime, celestial light, while its title, *Power Break,* refers to extinguished light. Hence, the interaction between the poem's content and its title creates an ironic paradox, one that agrees well with the aesthetics and ideology of metaphysical poetry (as well as with the aesthetic credo dictated to poetry by the literary school of American New Criticism).

Aesthetically, a paradox bestows upon the text potency that consists of tension, one that reinforces the poem's persuasive vitality.

By enlisting both the aesthetics and the ideology of metaphysical poetry, Asher Reich's poem stretches the "aesthetic agenda" of Hebrew poetry of the sixties without, however, "exiling" itself from it or challenging it too daringly. Reich offers to Hebrew poetry of the sixties his original, exquisite sound, one that is both poetically complex and artistically appealing.

Another poem by Asher Reich will again prove his affinity for the aesthetic and ideological agenda of seventeenth-century metaphysical poetry. Reich's attraction to metaphysical poetry is a conspicuous feature of one that pushes to the extreme. However, he still displays a modest, quite subdued, "meek" (but still *in esse*) "commitment" to the "aesthetic ticket" of Hebrew poetry in the sixties, the one dictating aesthetics of austerity, simplicity, and understated tones in theme, diction, and rhetoric. Reich's poetics attempts to reach a delicate balance between the religious and sexual themes of metaphysical poetry and the restraints of the aesthetics of austerity. Quite often, though, he sacrifices his commitment to aesthetics of austerity on the altar of metaphysical poetry and its plentiful richness. The poem "Another Voyage," like the previous poem, demonstrates Reich's ability to navigate carefully between the two conflicting poles to which he is committed: Hebrew poetry of the 1960s and seventeenth-century English metaphysical poetry. The following poem attests to Reich's desire to "reconcile" those two contradictory inclinations, to create a delicate balance between the two, and to maintain his place among the poets of his generation.

Another Voyage, One Lyrical Line Longer
And at night I am encountered by dreams, and in one
    dream, a woman,
An ancient goddess, at dim twilight, is ascending towards me

Like from within the water, a hummer is budding, dawning
    inside me
Her beauty turned into my wings, turned into the light of
    the world
And her heart that was hovering with me over the roofs,
Casted, as I woke up, a dense wall (and falsehoods)
Through which I have not gone anymore, nor did another
    man
From that murky, bleak barrier, from that somber, dismay
    obstacle,
I keep pecking, like a bird, one recollection
After another recollection.

The nocturnal scene that opens the poem creates a mysterious, dreamlike atmosphere that is familiar not only in Gothic and Romantic literature but also in metaphysical poetry. The ancient goddess associated with water (a traditional erotic element) evokes the image of an ancient goddess of fertility. The goddess of fertility (named *Asherah/Ashtoret* in the Hebrew Bible, for a tree that symbolized fertility and was worshiped through sexually oriented rituals), who carries strong sexual connotations, appears in a dim, misty twilight and ascends from the water, echoing the myth of Venus, the goddess of love and beauty who was born from the foam of the sea[26] (again water, associated with sexuality). According to Freud's theory of symbols, the act of rising, or ascending, is associated with sexuality (the ancient goddess in the poem is rising toward the narrator, ascending from the water like Venus, the goddess of love). The verb to ascend, to rise, to mount, in the Bible is also associated with sexuality. Reuben, for instance, is scolded by his father, Jacob, for having sexual intercourse with one of Jacob's concubines: "For when you ascended your father's bed, you brought disgrace—my couch he mounted" (Genesis 49:4). In Song of Songs, the female beloved is in these terms: "Who is the one who ascends from the desert, embracing, caressing her beloved" (8:5; see also 3:6). The visage of the goddess also introduces a certain religious, divine element. Thus, the poem fuses sexuality, mystery, spirituality, and religion, a mixture that harks back to metaphysical poetry.

The phrase "Like from within the water, a hummer is budding, dawning inside me" creates a sense of ambiguity (another manifestation of metaphysical poetry) from its association both syntactically and thematically with the earlier image of the goddess ascending from the water. It also, beyond the touch of ambiguity that it produces, suggests a union between the goddess and the narrator, a strong sense of sexual interaction, as in the Bible: "Hence a man leaves his father and mother and clings to his wife, so that they become one, united flesh" (Genesis 2:24). Since the union not only is of an erotic character but also carries religious, mystic, cosmic connotations, it further enhances the poem's ties to metaphysical poetry.

The union between the goddess and the narrator attains a higher level in the next two lines of the poem:

Her beauty turned into my wings, turned into the light of
    the world
And her heart that was hovering with me over the roofs.

Again, both thematically and syntactically, the two subjects, "her beauty" and "her heart," can relate to either the erotic goddess or the hummer that is "budding, dawning inside" the narrator. This double ambiguity reinforces their erotic-cosmic union. Their hovering "over the roofs" produces a mystic atmosphere and a sexual sense from the combination of two allusions. The mystic allusion suggests the paintings of Marc Chagall in which people, animals, and objects hover over roofs. It gains an erotic-sexual quality as well when one recalls Chagall's famous painting in which a bride and a bridegroom hover over the roofs. The erotic allusion sends us back to the Bible

A Goddess Shrouded by Shadows

where King David lusted after Bathsheba: "Late one afternoon, David rose from his couch and strolled on the roof of the royal palace; and from the roof he saw a woman bathing. The woman was exceptionally beautiful" (2 Samuel 11:2).[27] The reference to the roof in both the poem and the biblical text also echoes sexuality: the roof means a hovering that stands as a metonym for sexuality. In Freudian theory, hovering symbolically relates to sexuality, to an erotic inclination. Thus, the artistic allusion (Chagall), the psychological interpretation (Freud), and the biblical allusion create a strong atmosphere of sexuality with a mystic touch (hovering over the roofs is at odds with the rules of reality and, therefore, it evokes a sense of mystery). All these observations are further corroborated by the line

"Her beauty turned into my wings, turned into the light of the world." "Her beauty" carries erotic connotations that are connected to the mystic or celestial qualities of the unrealistic scene in which the narrator grows wings. Since hovering (associated with wings) on the part of a mortal human being is by definition of a mystic or celestial character, the act of hovering is also a sexual symbol, as previously explained. The words "the light of the world" can be easily connected to Kabbalah (Jewish mysticism), in which the light of the world is a central concept. Indeed, the two leading books of Kabbalah (probably from the twelfth century) are entitled *Sefer Habahir* (The Book of Light/Bright) and *Zohar* (Brightness). For instance, Kabbalah uses the concept of the world's ancient light, the Torah letters, as an intricate combination of the Godly light, *Ha'or haganuz* (the hidden/latent light), and more. Indeed, the very beginning of the Creation in the Bible focuses on light: "God said, 'Let it be light,' and there was light" (Genesis 1:3). Kabbalah also stresses mystical sexuality, such as "the sacred (sexual) union" between God and the nation of Israel.[28] The allusion to Kabbalah, detected in "the light of the world," brings together the poem's two leading themes: divine presence and sexuality. Both of them are equally prominent in metaphysical poetry.

Thus, the reader encounters a complex interaction in which mystic/celestial/cosmic (as well as religious) connotations are joined and linked to erotic connotations—biblical, artistic (Chagall), psychological/Freudian. The poem attains a dreamlike, misty, sensual quality, leading to a climactic ending.

Yet in the next verse, the complex cluster of allusions collapses into a bleak, dark, dusty abyss:

And her heart that was hovering with me over the roofs,
Casted, as I woke up, a dense wall (and falsehoods)
Through which I have not gone anymore, nor did another man.

The narrator's awakening from that lofty mysterious, sensual dream is painful and frustrating. As the Bible aptly put it: *"lifney shever—ga'on"* ("prior to a calamity—arrogance," Proverbs 16:18). The awakening, agonized narrator resembles the mythological Icarus, whose attempt to ascend to the heavens doomed him to a deadly downfall. This may be interpreted as a warning to all those whose hubris impels them to rise above the human capacity of mortals. The thorny, rough, harsh awakening from the dream is comparable to the expulsion of Adam and Eve from the Garden of Eden. What is left then is a blocking wall, a bleak barrier, and an insurmountable obstacle.

And the narrator? He who in his dream was like a celestial goddess, like a mystic bird, hovering over the roofs and filled with elevated, heavenly cosmic yearnings flooded by sweeping sexuality, now awakes from that celestial dream to find himself metamorphosed into a broken-winged bird. And the divine dream turns into dirt, dust, a pile of dung, from which the once heavenly bird (the narrator in his dream) is pecking at bleak, bitter bits of recollections. The mysterious, exquisitely sensual experience is translated into a somber, pitiful, painful, dilapidated reality. The narrator and the goddess were together transformed into one heavenly bird, hovering over the roofs, soaring to heights of spellbinding sexuality. Once the narrator's dream is over, however, that heavenly bird turns into a gray, gloomy bird attempting in vain to resurrect the recollections of its paradisiacal existence, now forever lost.

Asher Reich is a remarkably adept poet. Like a formidably skillful juggler, he keeps balls in the air without dropping them: the ball of aesthetics of austerity and the ball of metaphysical poetry, with its contradictions, complexity, and elaborate conceits. But, such aesthetic juggling comes with a price. In Reich's poetry, the price is stretching to the very limit the boundaries of aesthetics of austerity in order not to be exiled from the other "promised land" of meta-physical poetics. Nevertheless, that price seems worth paying, especially in view of the fact that the citizen of those two conflicting aesthetic "promised lands" keeps his literary loyalty to both without offending either.

The Poetry of
Asher Reich

An Anthology

SHOTS
Two Poems
In memory of Robby

I

No soldier shoots twice
at the same figure
except the shortsighted.

No soldier thinks twice
about the shot figure
except the slow thinker.

[Free translation from the Yiddish]
No man steps twice
into the same slime
except the slime fans and the pigs.

An honor guard near the open gate
fires a memorial-volley into the air.
What does a soldier see in the air?
What does he think?

Under heaven's clipped wings
nothing is permanent
nothing is the same thing
and all things are one,
that's life.

AP

Doomed Is the Bloom

2
Shooting and Burying

Steel and rust
and very close to the dead we lived
with each day the State
questions itself more.

Shooting and burying
for a spirit that passed here, is
from house to house rust passes
eating street after street
under a sky with clipped wings
the land too narrow to hold itself.

Shooting and burying
stupidly letting us get forgotten
remember as a Jew knows how to remember
from inside forgetting from inside the rust
we shall remember growing old with Time
who is kind to those who remember.

Translated by Vivian Eden

Desire Is Long-Distance Running

Desire is long-distance running,
crossing pits, leaping walls,
past hurdles,
sometimes a delectable landscape.
Alternately you open and close,
somersault as in gym exercises.

The soul and the body run in parallel paths
and dream in long jumps,
land on quicksand and disappear
while our blood approaches and retreats
in a butterfly stroke,
sometimes breaking old records.

Desire is long-distance running.
Sometimes you dream in the full light of words
on the summit of promise,
not knowing you've passed the holiest love,
that even the Olympic soul cannot touch.
Suddenly it grabs me like a pole and vaults.

The Book

When I moved recently, I suddenly found
my forgotten Bible:

A Bar-Mitzvah present, the only thing
I took with me when I deserted the home of my youth
for forty years in the desert.

I leafed through the book: some pages stuck together
as in a classified secret. Cain, of course, is still murdering his
    brother.
For every murder, two other brothers sprout up in the field.
Goliath takes off his armor and goes out to lunch

From his eternal battle with the little Israelite.
The Philistine's head is already adorned with rubber bullets
like kinky curls. The first astronaut.
Elijah shoots up in a storm to heaven in a regular launch.
Locally made UFO's sail in the skies of Ezekiel.

I continue skimming: the pages had already blackened with
    blood,
gory wars that continue on their own.
Only the sins remain like white stains, prophets
disappear from the book to prophesize far away. Kings
escaped to the Diaspora. Angels flew back to the caves of
    the firmament.
From his couch, God sadly ascended and turned out our
    light.

Translated by Karen Alkalay-Gut

Snapshot

She wakes,
oh, now she's rising.
Her height unfolds endlessly,
her eyes lighten—
oh, God, she's really up.
Measureless her height extends.
Stand still, says the angry wind, stand—
you won't miss a thing.

Suddenly she walks off.
Oh, now she's really leaving.
Her feet ignite the wind—
oh, God, she's really running!
Stop, the tired wind whispers, stop.
Don't do a thing.

Translated by Karen Alkalay-Gut

Portrait of a Pining Gloom

Not with the Greatest of Ease

My dog got sick.
I dreamt he died.
I buried him in the field

he loved most, near the rubbish pile
where he usually saw to his bodily functions
great and small
not with the greatest of ease.

If there's a Paradise for dogs, there shall he rest.
There shall his pure and holy senses be
a fit substitute for soul. And if there's a large bone
free, let it be set in the splendor of his lovely mouth
as symbolic equipment to whet his sharp teeth. A fig tree
not far from his heavy feet will delight him excite him

to deposit there his functions many times daily
as the vet decreed. And, if possible, maybe a small
garden for him alone, with gorgeous plants, wonderfully wild,
of the sort he so loved to trample when alive. Then it would be
just the natural place he could stay
a dead dog complete and with the doggy submission
he was trained to not with the greatest of ease since his youth.

Translated by Vivian Eden

Our Blood Is the World's Petrol

The day passes. We've gained some time.
Our days pass by in trash dreams.
Once I knew a boy
who waited for his life
and found his death.
His death
leavening
was a warning shot to me.

A dozing generation that awaits a miracle.
Waits in vain to the ends of its strength.
Wait. Maybe somewhere
in the ground of the seventh heaven
the best of our pilots
will discover cosmic oil
our blood is the world's petrol.

Translated by Karen Alkalay-Gut

Haifa in Winter

Haifa in winter is a Japanese woodcut.
Silken rain, the softest of rains, waits for me there,
the white moth sleeps in the damp bushes
and from the puddles a fountain of fantasies rises like a mist.
Haifa in winter floats on air with the buoyancy of clouds
and sometimes the horizon is a rice paper sail.
Then the sun-stained evening comes
like a gash in the belly of the city.

Translated by Karen Alkalay-Gut

A Distant Landscape Mistily Hovers Above

Revenge

The heroic rooster woke me up,
crushed my sleep with the boots
of his cock-a-doodle-doo.

But I smiled as I recovered.
This very evening,
the cock will be my supper.

At night I was visited by flocks of his crows.
Sunless in me rose
his red cockscomb.
The cock and I are one.

Translated by Vivian Eden

Loom Loneliness

A Lonely Woman

A lonely woman
is a bit of a woman
and a lot of loneliness. Only the sharpest eye discovers her
at best and at worst as she knits and purls
in books and out
the motions of her heart
just a bit for herself
and for others a lot
and the length of her loneliness even she doesn't know.
As she walks down the street
just the street walks beside her.
Just the perfume of loneliness
announces her coming.
Mostly, she meets herself in a tired mirror
or a familiar, shabby dream like a faded photo.
Sometimes she falls in love with a poem.
Her hometown is sad and cold,
and if she lives here in this neighborhood
she has a sea that receives her
with ripples and understanding.
Perhaps for her the quiet waves
will suddenly reveal
spring, a lucky season.
A lonely woman, mostly her soul,
tired of fingering Penelope's hope
voicelessly conjures all her loves,
performs a summer magic
as if still in her prime.
Can anyone see her unraveling herself?
And at night she waits to be saved from her stillness.
She makes her own bed,

she makes her own grave,
to rest in space, to sleep on her bed,
and her fingerdream sleeps beside her.
And the shudder passing through her
is wind and darkness
coming and going
as if they had never been.

Translated by Vivian Eden and Karen Alkalay-Gut

This Plenty

What has this plenty given you—
a full belly? Color in your face?
For the soul is ravenous and will not fill up.
It comes from the body's heaviness, from bitter four,
this obsessive plenty that evaporates in the sun.
What did it give and what could it possibly give?
Those who are found under the ground
know and acknowledge the wasted land above it.

The wasted land is plentiful the grass is plentiful
the mountains are plentiful the hills are plentiful.
When a boy and when grown
I knew not what it was that always blooms
under the ground, under the root,
and what is guarded behind the forehead.

All clocks lead to time
and time is not on our side.

Translated by Vivian Eden and Karen Alkalay-Gut

Sheet

Pure and white as I am I have no part in the dark plots
of lovers. All that I feel on my surface will come from flesh or
through sweat and sperm in the transparency of nighttime.
    A dumb voice
adhered to me like tears. A hair sheds onto me. Air implodes
    into me.
I crease and soil easily and will also hold no
grudge. For this is my purpose: much life spills into me
and from material like me they make flags of surrender or
    devotion.
Those who lie on me to sleep, to rest, to dream and to be
    cured
like those who come to me in love's pleasure and sigh rest
from the release that is in passion always conceal why they
    would conceal,
so I won't see their lives precisely realized. The skin of time
shines in me and passes over me musing on the ceiling's
    changing
colors. And when I am replete with worlds
living and bright in my infinite two meters,
suddenly I'm gathered me up, folded and thrown
into the dizzying laundry which burns my skin and innards
legally to erase it all, there the little I knew is wrung from me
and I'm like an infant unfurled to the world anew
pure and white as I am
and without any memory.

Translated by Vivian Eden

Poem from a Town in the Middle of Nowhere
The night train stopped crying.
The engine's soft eye
hid behind the steam
of its mouth.

The snake of carriages was like my train of thought.
No one was to be waiting for me
in this shabby station. A small town the name of which
is no citizen of my memory's labyrinth.
Perhaps that's why I suddenly decided to commune

with a violent night the likes of which I'd not yet known:
darker than the Valley of the Shadow ever
was. My tired body was tensed to rest here
a night. The hour was late
even for a solitary soul like me,
owner of all the empty hours. I alighted

from the train. Wind growled at me like a grieving bear.
The ugliness of the ugly blew all around. Through
the filthy vomit of the rain I could see
the day ash sighing on the shivering
skeletons of trees. The station emptied
and at my feet heavy earth breathed.
The country road blanched with cold. I entered
the hall which posed as a café, awaiting a taxi
that froze on the way. Cup after cup of coffee I drank,
in cunning camouflage of patience, accompanying the wall
clock's hand and the sirens of the wind. The hour was late
even for a solitary soul like me,
owner of all the empty hours. On my chair I dozed

into a dream: white angels like snow descended
and encircled me, bore me away to my childhood's one
   snowfall,
to my mother in Jerusalem: "Why have you come back so
   late, my son?"

Translated by Vivian Eden

Listen to Me Deaf Love

Listen to me Deaf Love
and I will tell you what I
feel from beyond your scintillating silence
and what I knew to feel without you
in the roots of the heart that have already whitened
like my mother's hair.

Listen to me stubborn obsession
and I will tell you who I
am, waking with you nightly
and what I would be without you
in the silent darkness of the light.

Love with light feet, you are
a life prisoner to me. Where are you
exactly when you sleep by my side?
What was near to the eye
like a remote desire that has lost its way
blossomed in your absence.
Go thee on your distant way, my desire,
and become a singing sea shell
that my love may hear through you
the throbbing of my heart.

Translated by Karen Alkalay-Gut

Forgettings

Jerusalem has forgotten me,
my entire youth a citizen
of her right arm.
My right arm
threw holy stones, every Sabbath
on passing cars.
In the mornings, every weekday
I bound with black thongs
a black box
on my left arm.

Jerusalem has forgotten us
her right arm
outstretched
now a monstrous body:
a great flock of artificial
limbs, anointed with black
messianic oil from Ophel.*
Thus they live, yesterday on their shoulders
as phylacteries between their eyes
and each of Jerusalem's stones,
a city embryoed together,
weeps over our silence.

In Jerusalem my right hand
is forgotten and the shadow of my tongue,
when I opened one of her hundred gates
with arms thirsting for the world,

Ophel: bleak, somber darkness. In the Bible, Ophel appears mostly in the book of Job, in relation to Job's agony.

my eyes shed large drops of fog sharp as blades.
The oil of twilight falls on Jerusalem
gone black within the walls and without,
sunset to sunrise a fateful rustle.
Only her lovers behold
the black jewel of her time
in death's pale nose.

Translated by Vivian Eden

Fortune Cookies

And again your eyes face a journey:
a distant song ignited them.

And the melody rises from the sea window:
Tide blighted yearnings
pull from a far place

that reveals fates. Women mostly know
how to distill from this a spark of vision:
they deck themselves in the murmur,
longing leaps across their faces.

You too,
upholster yourself in eagerness
don some sort of renewal
in the sweet and sour air.
The sea debris—coral wishes

sprinkling with cruel generosity
days of slanted expectations.
And again the inevitable temptation
to distance-echoes,
a hankering for the unknown
and wishes folded in your pocket like hankies.

This is the human: aspiring to the concealed,
indifferent to the revealed and submissive to all
the peddlers of hope,
the whisperers of delusion
the meddlers with the stars

it is not they who will nobly substitute
for the hidden days raked from our hands.

Translated by Vivian Eden

Patches

The universe has vanished. Only the sun
still remains. In silence
it wakes the emptiness.
Thus Mr. Silberman dreamt 1944.

An undestroyed past pieced with patches
of forty two years,
after a life-day in the Shoah* film.
That night the dream returned—

Water came back to life in a cloud
and fire in ash again revived.
Unfinished death
wrapped him like a wounded coat.
He woke mid-nightmare.

And with confident clarity, slowly put on
his Treblinka clothes, shaved with care,
made his bed, opened the gas, and
peaceful and sure went back to bed.

Translated by Karen Alkalay-Gut

Shoah: Holocaust.

New York: First Swim
As always, like at first, it began with the water.

Max Ernst's* blind swimmer
rose from the river, sodden with longings

for his dry-land life; escaped from all
the depths of his time, as if shaking off
his immortal waters. I saw his

centrifugal body
shake plutonium into the water. I saw too
how the waters thirsted for your mouth
you who feared them.
The whole island raced like a rumor. You too

ran. Your soul also changed seasons
like the green nude of Central Park
that changed colors into autumn. And then
we crossed the sobbing Hudson to Jersey,
to the frozen future of America's dream.

Translated by Vivian Eden

*Max Ernst (1891–1976): a prominent German painter whose Surrealist works of art saliently consist of free associations.

New York: Second Swim

Through a lighted tunnel under the river
we came back to Manhattan. The city was

wrapped in nickel clouds. There we lost
the voices of the bread, far from the Land of Honey.
There your system couldn't take the load

of the sweetness of the city's cakes.
You vomited in Macy's. In Alexander's I bought
woolen underwear and got a long erection.
Inside us were glass passions as high as

the twin
towers.
My face in the clouds was some kind of autumn
sun, of the Atlantic skies.
The eyes of my eyes photographed it all.

Our tourist blood flowed and flowered —
and I long for quiet moments with the books in Rizzoli's.
You and I like a pair of bears from the advertisement
shuffled along with the human funnel of the Marathon.
At night we took a walk with Eliot's cats
and all your fears rusted entirely.

Translated by Vivian Eden

Lake Reflection of a Fir Forest

Winter Music
for Sarah Kirsch

Things that won't be believed: primeval silence
the hum of the dark, through which I heard the voice of the deep.
The weather's caresses: the wind, the forest, the world-cloud.

I picked black bears in the forest,
mostly fed them cherries
and their growls of hunger furrowed
the silence of the forest.

Far between the legs of trees
a deer, trembling, hears the sounds.
The magic carpet is a woolly cloud.

Sarah the poet sits alone in her room
and with cherried words is writing

a poem: "Red fox have you known me to
hurry scurry to the heights
to seek my heart's desire?"

Writing a poem on a wintry night
warms the spirit. Through fat clouds rumors
land dripping fat

that isn't the fat of angels. This wind that knows
rain's language—is music. Pearls of rain glisten
on windows. Listen, Sarah, to the fox's howl
tearing the heavens. The house dog pricks up
big ears like gum-tree leaves. I see above me
cracks of nightish day. Look, Sarah, how
the village drunks fly upwards now to the sky.

Translated by Vivian Eden

Under the Winter

In the bitter winter under the quilt
or the unstable sky
without your thighs and their solid might,
a fluorescent memory your only trace.

My hands and their impotence
warm themselves with longings
and buzz with great yearning
and loneliness drips from me like sweat.

My senses are in a state of emergency
until they fall into sleep
into the dreambow
whose arrows fly to vanished worlds.

I've been to those southern islands, among
half-naked mulatto girls. You appear underground
and pull me out to the cold of morning.
There's nothing new under the fog.

Translated by Vivian Eden

The Soul Tree

Of all the fruit my mother tried
to feed me I loved only

the imagination fruit. It has no scent
but its taste deeper than any knowledge keeps me alive.
Endlessly I heard mother talking in the courtyard

with her neighbors about the soul tree. I tried
to follow its shadows that weren't there and I didn't know
whether it was in heaven or on earth. My mother who never
   stopped respiring good sleep into me for my soul's rest

cooked me a story every bedtime: the soul tree grows
far away in the seventh sphere. My father only smiled to hear
her imagination baking me lullaby legends of a tree
big as the world with seventy-seven roots the size of cities.
One night I heard from her that only a child who is clean

of sin might perhaps on a night when the moon is full
see the shadow of this tree
where all the souls fly at night
to rest while we sleep. And if your sleep is restless
from doing wrong, your soul is lost within itself
longing for the tree: the cathedral of the Godly heart.

Translated by Vivian Eden

The Soul, Lonely Tree, Whispers a Hissed Lullaby

Harmony

Still night. I am still bound
to the XXII letters

as it fettered. Only thickened silence like this
can light me a single word
gleaming in its many sounds.

I see it down to the bone,
to the end of the root.
It suddenly doubles.
It is now two.

My voice's one ear
hears night's shadows
creeping along Hebrew grammar.
Before me on the page, three words.
In a moment there will be more.

Now the blue scent of moon
can be seen through them. Thus was I made
aware of the dark's inaudible
pain. Sun of the night. The words glow.
Now you emerge from your sleep to me
and come into the poem.

Translated by Vivian Eden

The History of My Heart

Like light I passed
through my loves

fast
fading
unknowing. Real

time is not in the sun or clocks.
Time is metaphysical beatings
of the human heart: another universe
teeming with corpuscles,

a hidden civilization
orbiting an invisible sun.
Oh, my world, alive and moving
in its spheres: emotional gravitation.

This is my heart's history, studded with
dates of love: dark ages of shameful
defeat, melancholy kingdoms vanished in a
renaissance of discoveries and conquests. Future spills
into present like blood, like imperial loneliness
rising and falling, ruling over me, over and over again.

Translated by Vivian Eden

The Sleep of Youth

The boy sleeps. His bed is upholstered with stones
like the abyss.
Even in his dreams his face is veiled in despair.
From afar, for a moment, he will see the sun:
his bride-to-be.

A stone's throw away
another boy sleeps
on a soft mattress
tasting for the first time
the round blinding sun:
a golden-haired girl.
Words from the dictionary: Dream. Sun.
Words from reality: Abyss. Stone.

And the night is like this poem—a galloping horse
bearing two riders
raising old dust on the road.
Beyond the flight of the stone birds,
the road is a forest. Grace is a goal.

Translated by Vivian Eden

Cable

Night. Jerusalem.
Thinking of you. Full stop.
Wait like a tree. Stop.
Planted on water
without you—dash—
don't wish. Miss me.
New line.
Forget the past.
Arise
and come.

Translated by
Karen Alkalay-Gut

No Telegram Can Either Tell or Convey Her Everlasting Sorrow

Good Morning

Good morning to the white ceiling above me
where the smoke of my dreams is absorbed like a secret,
good morning to the four walls of my room
that shuts out the crude noise of the street.
Good morning to the closet
that like me hates dress clothes and suits.
Happy is the bay window
that tells me night and day of light and dark.
Blessed is the double bedstead that held me,
blessed is the waterbed on which I lay
and which always sates my thirst for dreams.
Blessed my slippers, that lead me through my room.
Good morning to all who rise early
not knowing what the day will bring.

Translated by Vivian Eden

Words to a Picture

This is my beloved,
the one on the right is
her brother who fell in the Lebanon war.

The one on the left is
her last lover
before I came
into the picture.

She is hugging them hard
as if she knew she would lose them both.
From the side, her mother regards them.
Her face looks like a browned cake
that time baked on too high a flame.

Translated by Vivian Eden

Landscape: No Place for Softness

Poems from Iowa City
To Chaim Pesach

In a place I came to live
an anonymous season

refreshed from the heavy, fevered skull
of the Levantine sun
I got entangled in a summer's tail you couldn't see the end of.

Had it chased me all the way here
from my home? Here on Iowa's titanic plains
September committed suicide with African heat.
My face filled with third-world summer.

It's a sun that glories across the limitless cornfields
lighting far and wide prejudices, secondhand fears.
And it's an ironical sun to paint a sky so white
in the bright brass of future. A sun that turns
a dreamy river to a shattered mirror and spurs
it along, without nuances, without wind.
At the dimming of the water, at the fading of the day
in the place where I came to be a quiet season,
patient in this plain, I still await
the fine nighttime light of the Middle West,
await, like the river, the wind that speaks rain.

With a yellow corn face
fall burst out. And it was different.

Translated by Vivian Eden

On His Death

At breakfast I spread
memory on a sliced roll
upon reading in the paper of "his untimely
death," as if death had a time of its own.
And he was the one who had said after years
that we hadn't met (I asked him: What are
you doing these days)—"For a year now I've been preparing

My death!" he whispered to me, glancing
quickly around. I didn't really understand
and suggested with a smile: "Slow down, don't rush!"
His hand vanished like a chameleon into his jacket and
    the movement

looked fraught with significance. Maybe he wanted to show
    me
proof, a medical certificate or something like that.
In mid-movement his hand stuck in his inner pocket
like someone who forgot what he wanted or remembered
    something else.
"I have lived like a pig and I want to die like an angel"
he declared to the rustle of his hand pulling out of the jacket
    lining.

Cheerfully he handed me a cigar and before we parted
a kind of smile of greater closeness crossed his face
and it occurred to me that in the coal bin of his life
he had devoted himself to the higher levels of our
    consciousness.
With the kitbag on his back he receded

and my morning coffee which has meanwhile got cold
I now sip slowly, slowly, in his memory.

Translated by Vivian Eden

I and They

I am visited by a dream of those who circle
there above us taking stock of the world's assets.
I don't envy them their loneliness,
I've more than enough of that,

or even their rare privilege of seeing
all we've been spared this time around.
I don't grudge them the luck of a weightless body.
I have enough hovering of my own
and like the astronauts I too

am sometimes roped to my seat in the half-dark
and that's only half a metaphor.
Anyone who deals with art for its own sake
in a real way, not to say genuine,
learns quickly enough to live with his loneliness
and the wonders of his hoverings in the dark.

Nonetheless, every day, like, for example
this prosaic morning when the sun is seen
to open her legs generously
and I am granted a new sunrise,
my daily jealousy is immediately aroused
of those circling above me who are granted
more than one sunrise, day by day.

Translated by Vivian Eden

Oh, Lord, Did You Ever Envision Such a Doleful View?

The Flight Goes On

Childhood was the art of aviation in air.
Words from the prayer book glided in space, I saw
mingled voices of prayer rise up like a victim.
And when I lifted my head to the skies I heard my eyes:
here comes a kite from another planet.
The shtibelach* were homosexual doves' nests,
and I as an infant captured in an air pocket grew
with a sensibility rotten as a tooth.
At night, in dreams of instance, I flew
to the four corners of far away neighborhoods,

Shtibelach is a Yiddish word that relates to small houses in eastern Europe (especially during the eighteenth and nineteenth centuries) in which Jews convened to pray together. These houses were not formal synagogues.

crossing gates to another century,
passing within transient worlds of Eros.
Among the blind of the Lord I was as a visionary
under the agnostic firmament
and the wind damaged all the idols in me.
Above the clouds the flight still continues.
The room's spaces were spaceships floating in imagination's light,
a chance sailing to the faraway past,
now running before me with fifty memories.
For a moment I stop and count: two hundred and forty-eight
organs make a body. Six hundred and thirteen
commands* accompanied me there like wild shadows.
And how many organs made a soul like the photo album
of a God-persecuted child?

Translated by Karen Alkalay-Gut

*Six hundred and thirteen is the number of commandments necessary to follow in order to practice Judaism to its fullest.

Days Walk among Us Like Spies

The earth sings the chronicles of our lives.
In this land days walk among us
like spies. Night puddles
where the rain is absorbed in firefly glimmers.
The wind is a coop of clucking chickens.
The song of the earth feeds itself on blood sounds.
The rustling of trees, the susurration of grass like ancient lyrics.

For days I listened to the sounds of the earth
trying to decipher its language
in renewing Nature, its wintry anger
that always defeats us
even indoors.

For days I was trapped wondering what rustles
in its damp and swelling belly
when it sheds its skin like a snake
and dons new skin.
I stripped naked to the sounds of words
to recount events to myself.

Translated by Vivian Eden

Sisyphus

All he wanted was a quiet place
for himself, after wandering through Hades.
he was always a genial man,
but they saw him as a stranger, dark-skinned.

They didn't like his nose.
Their obvious hostility influenced the boulder
he rolled upwards to build a house.
The mountain scorned him. The boulder slipped from his hands
and they burst into laughter at his distress: "We said so

we always said this creature, this strange stranger,
was only good for trade. No one of his sort will build a home
and work with his hands. After all he's weak by nature
and so very different from us." Sisyphus heard in pain
the knife of laughter behind his back. The toxic
scorn poisoned his strength, and then he decided:

I'll show them just how right they are!

Translated by Vivian Eden

Notes

Michael Kovner

1. His father, Abba Kovner (1918–87), immigrated to Israel in 1946 and became a celebrated poet and novelist. He is well remembered for leading resistance fighters against the Nazis in the Vilnius ghetto and later from the forests.

2. See Michael Sagan-Cohen, introduction to *Michael Kovner, Paintings 1985–1995* (Givatayim: Eli Meir Press, 1995).

Fervent Love Forever

1. I discuss Nathan Zach's and David Fogel's poetics in the following studies: "When Nathan Zach Wrote Poetry for the First Time and Later" (in Hebrew), *Iton 77* 81, no. 19 (1998): 20–23; "Returning to Zach Means Returning to Basics" (in Hebrew), *Moznayim* 70, no. 5 (1995–96): 33–36; "The Aesthetics of Austerity: Nathan Zach," *DOMES (Digest of Middle East Studies)* 6, no. 3 (1996–97): 1–11; "Israeli Poetry: Between Bridled Sentiment and Exiled Sentimentality—The Case of Nathan Zach," *Modern Judaism* 8 (1998): 157–65; "The Correct Poem: A Study in Nathan Zach's

Poetry" (in Hebrew), parts 1 and 2, *Hadoar* 61, no. 26 (1982): 417–18; no. 27 (1982): 430–31; "Exposing Dynamics in Poetry: A Comparative Study in Two Poems by David Fogel" (in Hebrew), *Rosh* 4 (1979): 11–17; "The Aesthetics of Austerity: David Fogel," *DOMES* 4, no. 2 (1995): 12–23; "Debate vs. Debut in Nathan Zach's Poetry, or: Poetics of Poverty in Contemporary Hebrew Poetry" (in Hebrew), parts 1 and 2, *Hadoar* 71 no. 17 (1997): 19–23; no. 18 (1996): 18–20; "Only Now, As the Dust Has Settled: Hebrew Poetry in the Sixties" (in Hebrew), parts 1 and 2, *Iton 77* 19, no. 197 (1998): 34–39, 46; no. 201 (1998): 30–36; "Trends in Modern Hebrew Poetry" (in Hebrew), parts 1 and 2, *Hadoar* 78, no. 12 (1997): 17–19; no. 13 (1997): 22–28; "The Jar, Its Content and Between the Two: When Intricacy Covers Simplicity, and Vice Versa, in Modern Hebrew Poetry" (in Hebrew), *Apirion* 56 (2001): 42–51.

Some of the articles mentioned above are included in my books: *A Sense of Structure: Modern Hebrew and Biblical Literature* (in Hebrew) (Tel Aviv: University Publishing Projects, 1987); *From Wooded Meadows to Downtown Tel Aviv: Contemporary Hebrew Poetry* (in Hebrew) (Tel Aviv: Papyrus Publishing House of Tel Aviv University, 1996); *From Medieval Spain to the Land of Cinderella: Studies in Hebrew Poetry and Children's Poetry* (in Hebrew) (Tel Aviv: Tag Publishing House, 1998); *Pain, Pining, and Pine Trees: Contemporary Hebrew Poetry* (illustrated by Nachum Gutman) (Tel Aviv: Papyrus Publishing House of Tel Aviv University, 2000); *Love in the Back Seat: Hebrew Poetry in the Sixties* (in Hebrew) (Tel Aviv: Tag, forthcoming).

2. I coined the expression "aesthetics of austerity" in my article "The Aesthetics of Austerity: David Fogel."

3. See David Fogel, *The Collected Poems* (in Hebrew with introductions by Dan Pagis) (Tel Aviv: Makhbarot lesifrut, 1966), 7–31, 47. Unless otherwise noted, all translations are by Yair Mazor.

4. Ibid., 41–47.

5. See Yair Mazor, *The Triple Cord: Agnon, Hamsun, Strindberg: Where Scandinavian and Hebrew Literatures Meet* (Tel Aviv: Papyrus Publishing House of Tel Aviv University, 1987), 12–13.

6. All Fogel's narrative pieces, except the novel, have been published in one volume: David Fogel, *Takhanot Kavot (Extinguishing Stations)* (Tel Aviv: Siman Kri'a, 1990).

7. For more about Fogel's prose, see my monograph *Not by Poem Only: David Fogel's Art of Narrative* (Tel Aviv: University Publishing Projects, 1987).

8. I discuss the nature of Zach's revolt against Alterman in "Israeli Poetry." In this article I also discuss Zach's poem "I Hear Something Falling."

9. See Nathan Zach, "Reflections on Alterman's Poetry" (in Hebrew), *Achshav* no. 3–4 (1949): 109–22.

10. *Dictionary of World Literature,* ed. J. T. Shipley (Princeton, N.J.: Princeton University Press, 1972), 221.

11. *Princeton Encyclopedia of Poetry and Poetics,* ed. Alex Preminger (Princeton, N.J.: Princeton University Press, 1974), 357.

12. Ford Madox Ford, "Those Were the Days," foreword to *Imagist Anthology* (London: Chatto & Windus, 1930), xiii.

13. See Shimon Zandbank, "T. S. Eliot and the Hebrew Poetry" (in Hebrew), *Siman Kri'a,* no. 5 (February 1976): 179–89.

14. Ibid., 189.

15. Quoted in James Guimond, *The Art of William Carlos Williams* (Urbana: University of Illinois Press, 1968), 14.

16. Robert Pack, *Wallace Stevens: An Approach to His Poetry and Thought* (New Brunswick, N.J.: Rutgers University Press, 1958), 14.

17. Elizabeth Sewell, *The Field of Nonsense* (London: Chatto & Windus, 1952), 5.

18. *"Leil Sharav"* ("A Burning Heat Night"), in Nathan Zach, *Shirim Shonim (Various Poems)* (Tel Aviv: Hakibutz hame'uchad, 1974), 12.

19. *Dictionary of World Literature,* 221.

20. A detailed study of Zach's "nonsense" poetry can be found in Miri Baruch, *The Bitter Romantic: A Study in Nathan Zach's Poems* (in Hebrew) (Tel Aviv: 1982), 13–14.

21. Asher Reich, *Mare'h Makom (A Reference)* (Tel Aviv: Massada Publishing House, 1978), 13.

22. Unless otherwise stated, all quotations are from the JPS Hebrew - English Tanakh, 2nd ed. (Philadelphia: Jewish Publication Society 1999).

23. I discuss the aesthetic device (as well as the sophisticated fashion it serves the literary text's ideological message) of "selective allusion in my following article: Yair Mazor. "A Study of the Selective Use of Allusions in

Poetry: A Comparative Study in Two Poems by Daliah Rabikowitz and Yehuda Amichai" (in Hebrew), *Rosh* 2 (1978): 23–27, later published in my book *A Sense of Structure,* 92–97.

24. See *Princeton Encyclopedia of Poetry and Poetics,* 495–96. Metaphysical poetry evolved in England as exemplified in the work of John Donne (1572–1631). Metaphysical poetry bends to complexity of the aesthetic texture, and at the same time portrays love from a philosophical viewpoint, witty rhetoric, and paradoxical structures. In metaphysical poetry, a merger of religious feelings and eroticism is quite common.

25. I discuss the prominent role of the *mevasser* in a poem by the celebrated Hebrew poetess Rachel (Blobstein) in "Rachel's Art of Poetry: Between Modesty and Complexity," *Modern Judaism* 10, no. 2 (1990): 147–58. A revised version of that article appears as "When Simplicity Meets Complexity and a Scream Translates into Silence" in my book *Pain, Pining, and Pine Trees,* 87–94.

26. See Edith Hamilton, *Mythology* (New York: New American Library, 1969), 32–33.

27. I addressed the erotic connotations of the roof in a biblical context in "And after All, Love: The Poem 'Archimedah' by Asher Reich,"in *A Sense of Structure,* 127–35.

28. Gershom Scholem, *Elements of the Kabbalah and Its Symbolism* (in Hebrew; trans. from German by Yosef Ben-Shlomoh) (Jerusalem: Mossad Bialik, 1980), 131, 136.

Works Cited

Baruch, Miri. *The Bitter Romantic: A Study in Nathan Zach's Poems* (in He-
brew). Tel Aviv: Alef Publishing House, 1982.

Fogel, David. *The Collected Poems* (in Hebrew). With foreword by Dan
Pagis. Tel Aviv: Makhbarot Lesifrut, 1966.

_____. *Takhanot Kavot (Extinguishing Stations).* Tel Aviv: Siman Kri'a,
1990.

Ford, Ford Madox. "Those Were the Days." Foreword to *Imagist Anthol-
ogy.* London: Chatto & Windus, 1930.

Guimond, James. *The Art of William Carlos Williams.* Urbana: University
of Illinois Press, 1968.

Hamilton, Edith. *Mythology.* New York: New American Library, 1969.

JPS Hebrew -English *Tanakh.* Second Edition. Philadelphia: Jewish Publi-
cation Society 1999.

Mazor, Yair. "The Aesthetics of Austerity: David Fogel." *DOMES (Digest
of Middle East Studies)* 4, no. 2 (1997): 12–23.

_____. "The Aesthetics of Austerity: Nathan Zach." *DOMES* 6, no. 3
(1996–97): 1–11.

_____. "The Correct Poem: A Study in Nathan Zach's Poetry" (in

Hebrew). Parts 1 and 2. *Hadoar (The* 61, no. 26 (1982): 417–18; no. 27 (1982): 430–31.

_____. "Debate vs. Debut in Nathan Zach's Poetry, or: Poetics of Poverty in Contemporary Hebrew Poetry" (in Hebrew). Parts 1 and 2. *Hadoar* 71, no. 18 (1994) 19–23; no. 18 (1994): 18–20.

_____. "Exposing Dynamics in Poetry: A Comparative Study in Two Poems by David Fogel" (in Hebrew). *Rosh* 4 (1979): 11–17.

_____. *From Medieval Spain to the Land of Cinderella: Studies in Hebrew Poetry and Children's Poetry* (in Hebrew). Tel Aviv: Tag Publishing House, 1998.

_____. *From Wooded Meadows to Downtown Tel Aviv: Contemporary Hebrew Poetry* (in Hebrew). Tel Aviv: Papyrus Publishing House of Tel Aviv University, 1996.

_____. "Israeli Poetry: Between Bridled Sentiment and Exiled Sentimentality: The Case of Nathan Zach." *Modern Judaism* 8 (1988): 157–65.

_____. "The Jar, Its Content and Between the Two: When Intricacy Covers Simplicity, and Vice Versa, in Modern Hebrew Poetry" (in Hebrew). *Apirion* 56 (2001): 42–51.

_____. *Love in the Back Seat: Hebrew Poetry in the Sixties* (in Hebrew). Tel Aviv: Papyrus Publishing House of Tel Aviv University, 2001.

_____. *Not by Poem Only: David Fogel's Art of Narrative.* Tel Aviv: University Publishing Projects, 1987.

_____. "Only Now, As the Dust Has Settled: Hebrew Poetry in the Sixties" (in Hebrew). Parts 1 and 2. *Iton 77* 19, no. 197 (1996): 34–39, 46; no. 201 (1996): 30–36.

_____. *Pain, Pining, and Pine Trees: Contemporary Hebrew Poetry.* Illustrated by Nachum Gutman. Tel Aviv: Papyrus Publishing House of Tel Aviv University, 2000.

_____. "Rachel's Art of Poetry: Between Modesty and Complexity." *Modern Judaism* 10, no. 2 (1990): 147–58.

_____. "Returning to Zach Means Returning to Basics" (in Hebrew). *Moznayim* 70, no. 5 (1995–96): 33–36.

_____. *A Sense of Structure: Modern Hebrew and Biblical Literature* (in Hebrew). Tel Aviv: University Publishing Projects, 1987.

_____. "A Study of the Selective Use of Allusions in Poetry: A Comparative

Study in Two Poems by Daliah Rabikowitz and Yehuda Amichai" (in Hebrew). *Rosh* 2 (1978): 23–27.

———. "Trends in Modern Hebrew Poetry" (in Hebrew). Parts 1 and 2. *Hadoar* 78, no. 12 (1997): 17–19; no. 13 (1997): 22–28.

———. *The Triple Cord: Agnon, Hamsun, Strindberg: Where Scandinavian and Hebrew Literatures Meet.* Tel Aviv: Papyrus Publishing House of Tel Aviv University, 1987.

———. "When Nathan Zach Wrote Poetry for the First Time. And Later" (in Hebrew). *Iton 77* 198, no. 19 (1997): 20–23.

Pack, Robert. *Wallace Stevens: An Approach to His Poetry and Thought.* New Brunswick, N.J.: Rutgers University Press, 1958.

Preminger, Alex, ed. *Princeton Encyclopedia of Poetry and Poetics.* Princeton, N.J.: Princeton University Press, 1974.

Reich, Asher. *Mare'h Makom (A Reference).* Tel Aviv: Massada Publishing House, 1978).

Scholem, Gershom. *Elements of the Kabbalah and Its Symbolism* (in Hebrew). Translated from German by Yosef Ben-Shlomoh. Jerusalem: Mossad Bialik, 1980.

Sewell, Elizabeth. *The Field of Nonsense.* London: Chatto & Windus, 1952.

Shipley, J. T., ed. *Dictionary of World Literature.* Princeton, N.J.: Princeton University Press, 1972.

Zach, Nathan. *Shirim Shonim (Various Poems).* Tel Aviv: Hakibutz hame'uchad, 1974.

Zandbank, Shimon. "T. S. Eliot and the Hebrew Poetry" (in Hebrew). *Siman Kri'a* no. 5 (February 1976): 179–89.

———. "Reflections on Alterman's Poetry" (in Hebrew), *Achshav* no. 3–4 (1949): 109–22.

Index of Names

Index of Titles and Subjects